Majella Connor

Patrick M. Devitt

IMMORTAL DIAMOND

FACETS OF MATURE FAITH

VERITAS

First published 1997 by
Veritas Publications
7-8 Lower Abbey Street
Dublin 1

Copyright © Patrick. M. Devitt 1997

ISBN 1 85390 317 5

British Library Cataloguing
in Publication Data.
A catalogue record for
this book is available
from the British Library.

Cover design by Bill Bolger
Printed in the Republic of Ireland by Betaprint Ltd, Dublin

CONTENTS

Foreword   7

Introduction: Helping faith to mature   9

1 Praying to the Father with thanks   14

2 Knowing God more clearly   22

3 Looking at life through the eyes of Christ   32

4 Building the future in hope   40

5 Changing radically under the Spirit's inspiration   50

6 Building community   61

7 Working for Christian unity   72

8 Sharing faith with all people   81

Textbooks consulted   90

Notes   94

DEDICATION

To the community of faithful catechists, both in Ireland and throughout the world, whose reflections have led to the publication of a General Catechetical Directory (1971) and to a new Directory (1997), in the hope that their work will allow the diamond of faith to shine its multi-faceted light into the hearts of God's people.

FOREWORD

This book is intended for people working in catechetical ministry, whether at home, in a parish or interest group, or in a school as a religion teacher. It draws inspiration from the General Catechetical Directory, in particular, its major idea that the function of catechesis is to help individuals and communities of believers to maturity of faith. The main thrust of the book is an analysis of the eight dimensions of mature faith.

A second focus is the establishment of links between this analysis and two major statements of faith, the Nicene Creed and the Catechism of the Catholic Church.

A third concern of the book is to offer some practical suggestions for parents, teachers and other catechists as they accompany their charges on the road to mature faith.

> I am all at once what Christ is, since he was what I am and
> This Jack, joke, poor potsherd, patch, matchwood,
>   immortal diamond,
>   Is immortal diamond.
>
> *Gerard Manley Hopkins, 'That Nature is a Heraclitean fire and of the Comfort of the Resurrection'*

INTRODUCTION

HELPING FAITH TO MATURE

The famous Scottish priest, John Dalrymple, in a retreat preached in Dublin during the 1970s, identified three styles of Christian faith commitment. A believer could be committed to the 'IT' of Christian faith – the institution, the visible structures. Alternatively (or, indeed, conjointly) one might be committed to the 'ISM' of Christianity – its ideologies, its theologies, its value systems. Finally, a person could be rooted in the 'HIM' of Christianity, namely, Our Lord Jesus Christ. While stressing that a balanced faith needs commitment at all three levels, Dalrymple nevertheless placed the emphasis on commitment to 'HIM'. In doing this, he was being faithful to the modern perspective. 'To whom are we committed?' is a question that has a thoroughly modern sound to it.

However, I should like to suggest an equally valid way of asking the basic question of belief today: 'To *what* are we committed?' Put in more detailed language, it runs like this: 'As believers in Jesus Christ what are we committed to doing, or being or becoming?' There is a slight shift in emphasis here, away from the object or content of our faith (what the medieval theologians called *fides quae*) towards the act of commitment at the heart of believing (what is sometimes referred to as *fides qua*). My emphasis will be on that whole range of activities[1] which express and confirm one's faith commitment to 'HIM', who is our Lord. I shall try to describe the richness of that process of being committed to Christ.

A careful reading of paragraphs 21-30 of the General Catechetical Directory suggested to me the following schema: a person of mature faith would be committed to praying with thanks, to knowing God more clearly, to looking at life through the eyes of Christ, to building the future, to changing radically, to building community, to working for Christian unity, to sharing faith with all people. All of these activities would be part of growing up[2] in the faith. Growth should be occurring in each of these dimensions of the faith, if it aspired to the status of mature faith. I do not claim either that this list is a comprehensive one or that these activities can ever happen in total separation from one another. Rather I suggest that, taken together, they reveal the richness of faithful living. They are a reasonably full statement of what is implied in putting one's faith commitment into practice. They could even be taken as a description of the 'practising Christian' (this phrase today often has a very narrow meaning, usually referring to attendance at liturgical functions). Faith is here likened to a diamond with many facets. Though each facet is linked to the others, it nevertheless deserves to be closely examined on its own.

In describing these various activities of a committed faith, I have deliberately chosen the participles of the verbs – knowing, sharing, changing etc. This is an attempt to highlight the fact that mature faith must, in some sense, be active. It must express itself in action. The New Testament puts it like this: 'Not everyone who says to me "Lord, Lord", shall enter the kingdom of heaven but he who does the will of my Father who is in heaven.'[3] In another place we read: 'Be doers of the word, and not hearers only, deceiving yourselves'.[4]

1. I want to explore what this doing (this activity) should consist of.

2. I also want to highlight some references to these dimensions of faith in the Catechism of the Catholic Church and also to show very briefly how these activities are referred to implicitly in the profession of faith made within the Sunday Eucharist, the so-called Nicene Creed.[5]

3. Finally, in the light of the new possibilities for education in modern culture, I want to suggest some ways in which catechists could foster these numerous 'faith-activities'.

The biggest difficulty, having named the many facets of an active faith, is to know precisely where to begin. There are three reasons for begining by considering faith as 'praying with thanks'.[6] Firstly, common parlance tends to equate practice of the faith with its prayerful, liturgical dimensions. This basic intuition should be respected. Secondly, the ritual of Baptism (whereby one is initiated into the faith) talks of the person becoming part of the priestly, prophetic and kingly ministries of Christ. It seems quite apt, therefore, to talk first of all about the priestly ministry, which involves 'praying with thanks'. The third reason for beginning here is that it enables us to follow a very traditional catechetical schema, that used by St Augustine, namely FAITH, HOPE and LOVE.[7] The model below will clarify the forthcoming analysis.

MATURE FAITH

FAITH (narrow sense)	1. Praying with thanks 2. Knowing God more clearly	PRIEST
HOPE	3. Looking through Christ's eyes 4. Building the future	PROPHET
LOVE	5. Changing radically 6. Building community 7. Working for Christian unity 8. Sharing faith with all	KING

This model could also be expressed as follows: A faith growing and developing to maturity has many interrelated dimensions, namely:

1. Worship – *faith as expressed in prayer and ritual*
2. Intellectual – *faith as understood and explained*
3. Prophetic – *faith as colouring one's vision of life*
4. Eschatological – *faith as generating the future*
5. Moral – *faith as lived out in one's values/decisions/life*
6. Socio-political – *faith as work for justice*
7. Ecumenical – *faith as relating us to fellow Christians*
8. Missionary – *faith as relating us to non-Christians*

The purpose of this analysis is ultimately a very practical one. It is to help catechists and religion teachers to identify the major long-term objectives[8] that should govern their catechetical work and their religion teaching. The General Catechetical Directory (21-30), talks about all the goals that catechesis is trying to achieve. The key idea here is 'maturity of faith'.[9] An analysis of this idea suggests the many functions of catechesis: 'If a person mature in the faith is one who does A, B, C, then catechesis should provide X, Y, Z.' That is the logic of paragraphs 21-30. The task now is to spell out that logic in some detail.

The work of catechesis ideally begins at birth. Parents are the first teachers of the faith. But what precisely can or should parents do? And are there special moments when they can encourage different facets of the faith? What contribution can be made to the maturing faith of primary schoolchildren, either in class by their teachers or in church or the school hall by the local priests?

A special advantage of dealing with the practical, visible side of maturing faith is that the educational encounter with religion in school involves a study of religion; so, describing faith in practical terms (in publicly accessible terms) should help us better to explore it. The religion teacher makes many contributions to the faith education of pupils in Catholic schools, both inside and outside the classroom. Through the examination and study in class of the eight dimensions of mature faith, the religion teacher is involved in a distinctive way in the faith education of the pupils. Through teaching religion in class, one major contribution of an *educational* nature is made to the ongoing faith education of the pupil. To reduce or limit the school's responsibility for faith education to what happens in religion class is to be unfair to the pupils, because they need a larger context for this work to be beneficial. It is also unfair to the religion teacher, who is thereby given the burden of a major responsibility without receiving adequate support. It is also unfair to the other teachers, since they are effectively *not* encouraged to play their own real and distinctive part in the overall process of faith education, through teaching their own subjects well. It is, finally, unfair to the school as an integrated system. No such system can afford to put too much reliance on any one of its elements, no matter how strong it may be.

1 *Worship Dimension*

PRAYING TO THE FATHER WITH THANKS

prayer + Ritual

See CCC 1122-26; 2559-65; also TYMB 116-117[1]

In the wake of liberation theology which stresses the link between faith and justice, and which calls for the involvement of believers in the complex world of social life and politics,[2] it may seem strange to begin this analysis with a recommendation to be 'praying with thanks'. However, even such a highly critical writer as Tissa Balasuriya allows that 'the internal spiritual life and the commitment to socio-economic liberation are not contradictory'.[3] He points to the example of Mahatma Gandhi, as a man whose 'deeper inner reflection [was] associated with a radical social commitment'.[4] We are not talking here about believers who are so heavenly-minded as to be of no earthly use. Rather, we are stressing that faith people need, not only a profound involvement in issues of community welfare and justice,[5] but also the pleasure of relaxing with God in silent prayer and creatively wasting time with their fellow believers in the liturgy.[6] *People need to take time to pray*

- The Nicene Creed is primarily an act of worship which ends in Amen. As well as being itself a prayer, the Creed also implies that the life of faith needs a prayerful dimension. It does this when it states that 'with the Father and Son he is worshipped and glorified'. In the General Catechetical Directory we read that a person mature in the faith 'is impelled to communion with God and with his brothers'(23). In other words, the religious 'communion with God' is tied to the socio-political 'duty of solidarity'. An analogy might almost be a married couple who cannot be divorced. Both the Jewish and the Christian traditions have always joined together prayer (the religious) and almsgiving

Praying to the Father with Thanks

(the social). The *Didache*, perhaps the earliest Christian catechism, explicitly links prayer and fasting.[7] The story of Martha and Mary in the Gospel is a story of the active person and the contemplative person. In so far as a certain priority was accorded by Jesus in this story to Mary, the contemplative one, it is perhaps permissible to begin with this dimension of mature faith.

Jesus invited his disciples to look at him and observe how he lived: 'Learn of me,' he said. When we try to apply this approach, by exploring his life of faith, we see immediately that he was obviously a man of action (he went about doing good). Equally obviously, too, he was a man of prayer (he was often alone in prayer on the mountains).[8] Each of these faith elements was allowed to thrive, and a wonderful balance was achieved. What resulted was a life of power and compassion, within which was cultivated and integrated a marvellous rhythm of activity and contemplation, each element feeding off the other, each flowing into and out of the other. All this can be seen in the Gospel story. A detailed analysis of chapter one of Mark's Gospel brings home this point very clearly. In verses 21-28, Jesus and his fellow Jews are listening to God's word and singing psalms in the synagogue. However, this does not prevent his actively healing a demoniac. Such power, such authority is actually seen as a new kind of teaching. Then, in verses 29-34, Jesus continues to heal, both in Simon's house and outside on the road. In verses 35-39, Jesus is on the mountain, communing in silent prayer with Abba. From this mountain he comes down to go further afield preaching and healing.

This is obviously meant as a model for the believing Christian. We, Jesus' disciples, are invited to model our faith lives on the rhythms of his – in which prayer is so central. This perspective is the one adopted by the General Catechetical Directory, when it says that 'catechesis must promote an active, conscious, genuine participation in the liturgy of the Church....

15

[Handwritten at top: We must reflect on our prayers and have silent time with God, personal prayer etc.]

The spiritual life, however, is not confined to participation in the liturgy… therefore, catechesis must also train the faithful to meditate on the word of God and to engage in private prayer'(25). In other words, just as our faith is communitarian as well as personal in nature, so too should be the prayer-life of a faithful person. Some specific suggestions are made here, especially with regard to liturgical prayer.

- Catechesis should **explain**[9] the meaning of the ceremonies. This corresponds to what used to be called, during the period of the catechumenate, a mystagogical catechesis, i.e. an exposition given to newly-baptised converts, in the period immediately after their Easter baptism and based on the symbolism of the rituals they had just experienced.

- Catechesis should form the minds of the faithful for prayer, for thanksgiving, for repentance, for praying with confidence, for a community spirit, for **understanding** correctly the meaning of the creeds.

A historical survey both of the catechumenate period and of medieval Christendom clearly shows that there is a very strong traditional link between liturgy and catechesis. This link is a dialectical one; it works both ways.[10] On the one hand, a preliminary instruction can lead to more conscious participation in the liturgy. This greater consciousness, in turn, can lead to a richer experience of 'living liturgy'.[11] Then again, liturgy, consciously celebrated, can generate new and richer insights into life and into the mysteries being celebrated.[12] In fact, it would seem that the main function of mystagogical catechesis was to draw out and formulate some of these developing insights. Thus, doctrine flowed from prayer. *Lex orandi, lex credendi.*

The Second Vatican Council talks of the liturgy as 'the summit towards which the activity of the Church is directed [it

[Handwritten at bottom: We must all partake in the liturgy which is the]

might even be translated 'the honours course']; it is also the fount from which all her power flows.'[13] The image of summit seems to suggest a high-point, but also the need to have a broad, firm base (the foothills of Christian life – the work of peace and justice). It also suggests that liturgy is what we are aiming at and that, perhaps, some people may take longer than others to get there (it is, after all, an uphill climb). This image, finally, suggests that everyone has to climb to the summit in order to have vision (the vision of what is practical) – in this sense the summit is also the source of power for action.[14]

The liturgical dimension of faith flows naturally from the need faith has to express itself in order to survive and develop. Later on, we shall see how faith needs to express itself in words, images and propositions – then we shall be concerned with faith and doctrine, with faith as knowledge and understanding which is clear enough to be communicated through talking and writing. We shall also see how faith needs to express itself in action (in moral behaviour, values and attitudes). For the moment, however, we are concerned with another form of expression – through symbol and ritual. Perhaps an analogy may make the point clearer. Faith is often likened to faithfulness and particularly to marital fidelity. Now married people often talk together, and discuss matters together and express their feelings and emotions in words. Likewise, they often do favours for each other, they are active in the service of each other, they express their bond in action. However, symbolic gestures, high-points and dramatisations are also essential for the healthy growth of a marriage relationship – birthday presents, a night out together, anniversary parties etc. – in short, celebration. Faith, too, needs celebration – celebration of what is, for the sake of what is yet to come.[15] Obviously, too, the worship dimension of faith will have a different profile depending on whether one is talking about young children, young adolescents or older adolescents and adults.

Immortal Diamond

[Handwritten annotation: *Parents are the first teachers in child's faith eg =*]

Let us now examine the worship dimension of faith from the perspective of a person brought for baptism as an infant by believing parents. In the ceremony of baptism, the parents are described as the first teachers of their child in the ways of faith. They are first in two senses; in time and in importance. Simply by being good parents they lay the human foundations of the faith life of their child. Long before the parents invite the child to kneel down and pray, long before they help the child to lisp the Our Father, they are already engaged in developing the faith life of the child. Their daily care gives confidence and hope to the child. Their reliable love invites love in return from the child. Their smiles draw forth the child's first act of faith. Their own reverence for each other and for the child lays down a sediment of reverence in the child's own heart. Their choice of religious art (crucifixes, pictures, cribs) and music (hymns and carols) can open the child's imagination to the wonder of God each day. Simple prayers said by parents at meal-time or before going to bed or on hearing bad news are the child's first lessons in the art of praying.

If parents are indeed the child's first teachers in faith, what about neglectful parents? All is not lost. There is always the chance of a grandparent or an uncle who is more diligent at prayer. Even older children, learning new prayers in school, can have an impact on the faith life of the very young child. Play-school teachers or baby-sitters who tell fairy stories with passion will introduce the young child to the deepest aspects of human experience (love and hate, life and death, failure and success, loss and gain, lost and found, breakdown and restoration). One of the most hopeful signs in recent years is the rediscovery of the human need for good story-telling. Learning to listen well to any story helps the young child to listen carefully to the greatest story ever told (God's own love-story, told in many different versions in sacred scripture). To respond, often with excitement, to well-told stories is perfect training for a child one day to rejoice and sing gratefully to God for his compassion. This is precisely what is meant to happen in liturgy.

[Handwritten margin note: How a child is introduced to Prayer in Primary School]

Praying to the Father with Thanks

But first the child has to learn the languages of prayer. All throughout primary school the teacher introduces the child to a wide range of public prayers (some biblical, like the psalms; others liturgical, like responses at Mass; others devotional, like the stations of the cross or the rosary). The teacher also leads the child into sung prayer, or mimed prayer, or dance prayer. The child is encouraged to pray not just out loud but even in the silence of her heart. The child is gradually encouraged to put her own words on some of her prayers. In such ways is the faith life and worship ability of the young child deepened and enriched.[16]

And what about ritual? Without a willingness to engage in ritual, there can be no real sacramental worship. As everybody knows who has had dealings with people joining strange religious cults, all human beings are naturally open to ritual. Children's play is highly ritualistic. They are especially pleased to do things over and over again. Ritual never bores them, in fact, it inspires them. By playing simple games with the child, parents can easily foster the growing child's ritual potential. By spending quality time with the child even a cynical parent can be converted to good ritual. Each family should develop its own intimate rituals of celebration and healing. There is no firmer base on which to construct a healthy sacramental practice later on in life. A child who has been happy with ritual at home and is introduced to the rituals of first confession and first communion at school can begin to share with greater ease in this new sacramental life. The playful work of the young child can grow into the celebratory work of the Church called liturgy.

Catechesis is a complex activity which involves the active participation of many different people. While parents are ideally the first catechists of each child, they are not the only catechists. Even as they prepare for the christening of the child they may well have met a member of the baptismal team of the local parish. This person, usually a parent like themselves, has a very important catechetical role: to encourage the parents to take seriously the responsibilities flowing from having asked for the child to be baptised; to explain the rituals and symbols of baptism; and to support the parents in their great act of faith. In another context altogether, the parish choir-leader can contribute much to the catechetical life of the parish. Careful selection of suitable hymns and chants can inject a divine sweetness into the liturgy. If there is a sensitive priest who plans parish liturgy in an imaginative way, if the parish church is bright and warm, if the people who pray and worship there are welcoming to all and sundry, then the growing child will easily integrate into the worship life of the local community. Then the parish will realise its true potential as the pre-eminent place for catechesis.[17] It will confirm and celebrate the often unsung efforts of diligent parents and grandparents, and the often unseen work of schoolteachers and chaplains.

The thirteen years spent at school are like thirteen colours in a rainbow. The spectrum of religion teaching between the ages of five and eighteen is shaded from a strongly catechetical to a strongly educational tone. The explicitly catechetical programme of the primary school (assuming some faith in each child and recognising the imitative nature of young faith) has to modify slowly during second-level schooling, in order to take account of the growing child's need for increasing independence and freedom of choice. Two major changes should occur in the worship life of the teenager. One has to do with freedom. Whereas primary school children are delighted most of the time to take an active part in school liturgies, as puberty progresses an inner change of heart can often accompany the great outer physical changes. The older teenager should, wherever possible, be free to go to *or* to stay away from school liturgies. The second change has to do with the way teenagers can best relate to worship, less by doing it than by studying it. That is why all the best religious education programmes and texts for senior cycle pupils place such an emphasis on the serious study of worship,[18]

Praying to the Father with Thanks

taking account of the older teenager's ability to reflect upon earlier sacramental experiences. In class at this stage the teaching objectives should be in the realm of knowledge and comprehension of the faith rather than in getting the teenager to practise the faith in worship. A teenager who has reached sixth year in school already has an assured status as a voting citizen. Teenagers should also have many regular opportunities to take critical stock of their religious faith and to begin freely to make it their own.

After such a promising foundation in faith education has been laid down in schools, it is lamentable that so few young Irish adults today have the opportunity to pursue seriously the education of their faith as they move into the workplace or pass through the halls of academia. Apart from those who enter seminaries or teacher education centres, most young adults are left mainly to their own devices if they wish to further their education in the faith. The work of faith development organised by the CYC and other such organisations has a strong worship dimension. Young adults are encouraged to create their own liturgies and to enliven the liturgies of their own localities. Often they are able to go on pilgrimage and thereby discover their identity as the pilgrim people of God on earth. Many young adults are introduced to Christian meditation and contemplation as they explore the lives of the great mystics. The fourth section of the Catechism of the Catholic Church is a gold-mine waiting to be excavated by all those who are keen to grow in prayer and worship of God.

At school =
- *Teenagers should not be forced to participate in Liturgies.*
- *They should be forced to practice their faith in worship.*
- *Teenagers should be allowed to make their own choices and form their own opinions.*

2

KNOWING GOD MORE CLEARLY

See CCC 429; 156-9; also *TYMB* 114

The teaching of religion in schools was once called RK (religious knowledge). This is understandable, given that schools are concerned with knowledge and religion can be explained and understood, at least to some extent.[1] However, the phrase 'religious knowledge' is not as simple as it appears at first sight. To know the catechism answer, to know Jesus Christ crucified, to know about your religion, to understand the faith, to know God – each of these could be regarded as a kind of 'religious knowledge'[2] and, while they all seem to be somehow related to one another, what poses problems is the *nature* of the precise relationship between them. For example, does 'knowing the catechism' come before 'knowing God'? To know Christ Jesus, is it necessary to understand the faith? Or is it the other way round? The distinction I referred to earlier, Dalrymple's threefold analysis of the object of faith as 'IT', 'ISM' and 'HIM', may help to bring some clarity into the confusion and, for that reason, I return to it now, in the context of a brief look at our history as a people of faith.

For most people today faith and religion mean the same thing. We just as easily refer to our faith as the Catholic faith and write in the official census forms that our religion is Roman Catholic. But it was not always so. Our earliest ancestors in faith, the early 'Christians', did not see themselves as belonging to a new religion. Many of them, if asked what their religion was, would have said they were Jews, and in keeping with this self-understanding they continued, even after becoming believers in Jesus Christ, to observe the religious customs and traditions of

Knowing God More Clearly

the Jewish religion. It is also interesting to note that it was often secular rather than religious language that they selected when describing their leaders – they called them elders, overseers and presbyters rather than priests. Even when, in the Letter to the Hebrews, Jesus himself is called the eternal high-priest, it is clear that the word 'priest' here has a metaphorical rather than a strictly religious significance, for Jesus was known to everyone as a layman within the Jewish religion.

When the early 'Christians' described themselves ('Christians' is, after all, a nickname given by outsiders, but eventually accepted by the believers) they preferred to use phrases such as 'followers of the way'. And when, from time to time, they met together in their own homes to celebrate what was specific to this way of life, to break Eucharistic bread and eat together, they never regarded this celebration as being separated from life and pertaining to some unknown sacred regions (connotations often associated with religion). The Eucharist, in fact, was understood by them to be a fellowship meal celebrating the breakthrough of the transcendent God into the very heart of ordinary secular existence. This activity of Eucharistic celebration was the supreme expression of the faith of these 'Christians', and that faith was neatly summed up in the phrase 'Jesus is Lord'. As Donal Murray puts it, the first Christian profession of faith was startling in its simplicity: "Jesus is Lord".[3] To borrow Dalrymple's terminology, we can say that they were clearly emphasising the 'HIM' aspect of the faith, their belief in HIM who has risen.

As the believing community developed through the ages and moved out from Jerusalem to the ends of the earth, the social, organisational and structural implications of the momentous paschal event at the heart of faith (the death/resurrection of Jesus) all had to be worked out over and over again.[4] The believers of subsequent centuries and of faraway places had to find new ways and means of living out the one faith in constant interaction with

23

new cultures and new worlds. Today, this process is called inculturation of the faith. It is a corollary of the process of incarnation, whereby God was made flesh in Jesus of Nazareth. When we are born into the Christian faith today our faith in HIM, who is our Lord, comes to us clothed in the accretions of almost two thousand years of religious tradition (what Dalrymple calls the IT and the ISM). The pearl of great price comes to us together with the whole field in which it is buried; sometimes it can be difficult to lay hold of the pearl (our faith) because the field (traditional religious practices, customs and insights) both conceals and reveals HIM in whom we believe.

If religious education were to concentrate on the IT and ISM[5] dimensions to such an extent that it overlooks or compromises faith-education (with priority given to HIM), it might lose touch with its ultimate foundations.[6] There is no question here of scorning our religious traditions and attempting to return to our origins. This would truly be a retrograde step, even if it were possible. It is rather a matter of evaluating our living tradition today in the light of the many traditions in which it has already been expressed and judging all in relation to their ultimate source – the resurrection of HIM, who is our judge. In this way we come face to face with Christ who is the root of our faith. It is he who gives meaning to and critiques the many religious traditions (the ITs and the ISMs) of our faith. Within such a perspective, one is at once a traditionalist and a radical. A traditionalist who is truly radical realises clearly that tradition is coextensive with the whole course of Christianity, and does not go back merely a century or two. Christian tradition is rather the constant reinterpretation and incarnation in each subsequent age and in each specific culture of the momentous paschal event, wherein the Father raised HIM from the dead.

Corresponding to Dalrymple's threefold analysis (IT, ISM, HIM) there are three kinds of religious knowledge: **factual, systematic** and **personal**. Factual knowledge is 'to know that something is the case'. It answers the 'what' question. Systematic knowledge answers the 'why' question. It helps us know the reason why something is the case. Personal knowledge occurs when we love or respect or trust another person. Whom do you know? The Irish language has many different words that translate into English as 'knowledge'. Irish distinguishes between 'fios', 'eolas' and 'aithne'. This, in itself, should alert us to the possibility of over-simplification when we talk of religious knowledge. However, it also suggests that the scope of this concept may be greater than seems at first.

1. While **factual** knowledge may not be everything in religion teaching, nevertheless it has its own place, especially in the context of primary schooling. This is where young people are told the stories of their faith and are introduced to a wide range of scriptural characters. The primary catechetical programme also introduces young people to the lives of the saints and to the saintly believers of modern times. It helps them to situate their Catholic faith in the specifically Irish context, and emphasises the importance of locality in the life of faith. All of this is essential groundwork for building up their factual and historical religious knowledge and eliminating their religious ignorance. Ignorance can hardly be bliss, when one is trying to grow to maturity in faith. All forms of religious ignorance should gradually disappear as the pupils grow and mature, e.g. ignorance of what our ancestors in the faith were like, ignorance of what is special to the other Christian traditions, ignorance of the values cherished by the great world religions and which are also dear to us Christians, ignorance of the contributions made both in the past and today to the development of humanity by committed Christians from every denomination.

2. Another kind of religious knowledge may be called **systematic** knowledge. It is an attempt to bring reason and

order to bear on the complex phenomenon of religion. It is an effort at interpretation of the facts. It is abstract, general, conceptual knowledge. Its main values are that it allows for clarity of thought, and allows one to explain in simple but accurate terms the meaning of one's faith. It allows believers to give a coherent account to others of the hope that lies within them. A mature Catholic believer would know, for example, why Christians use water in baptism, why the Mass is called a sacrifice, what constitutes the meaning of sin and reconciliation, why the Gospels are so called, why Jews and Christians say 'God calls us', why Jews pray at the Western Wall and feel aggrieved that most people refer to this as the Wailing Wall, why all Christians celebrate the Eucharist and why they understand it differently. The phenomenal success, even among second-level pupils, of the novel *Sophie's World* proves that many adolescents are quite capable of philosophical reflection. The religious education they receive in school should challenge them in accordance with this competence.

The pedagogical *skills* (stimulus variation, use of chalk-board, higher-order questioning, classroom management, use of texts and audio-visual media); the teaching *strategies* (teacher exposition, concept formation, concept extension, interpretation of data, narrative, problem solving, simulation, group-work, use of advance organiser); and the *meta-strategies* (experience-tradition and project work) which trainee religion teachers learn about are all meant to serve the process of systematic religious knowledge. Incidentally, both factual and systematic religious knowledge are, in principle, examinable. Whether the examination should be a state examination (like the Junior or Leaving Certificate) or a house examination (at the end of term in school) is another question altogether. It is best left as an open question for now.

3. The third kind of religious knowledge is **personal** knowledge. It relates not so much to IT or ISM as to HIM. When the Jews talked about 'knowing God' they didn't mean a dispassionate objective knowing such as would be implied in the phrase 'I know that God exists, and I know also what God is like – but now let me get on with living.' The Jews (and Jesus was a Jew)[7] understood knowing God to mean a life of interpersonal communion with God. It implied an activity of the whole person whereby one came more and more into contact with the transcendent in the midst of life. The emotions, the mind, the will, the heart but, especially, one's living justly day by day, all entered into this knowing. The Jewish scriptures used the image of married love to evoke this rich form of knowing. The Gospels and Epistles often refer to this knowing as FAITH *(pistis)*.

Within Catholic schools, the 'aithne' dimension of faith is the responsibility, not primarily of the religion classroom, but rather of the overall school community, since 'aithne' comes mainly from praying and doing justice. The more one knows, in this profound sense, the more one is challenged to knowing in the other senses too. Whether or not 'fios' and 'eolas', of themselves, can ever bring about this kind of 'aithne' is a moot question. The fact that Adolf Hitler always got first place in his religious knowledge examinations in school should counsel wariness here. Nevertheless, religion teachers will want to go far beyond the 'teach 'em the facts' approach immortalised by Mr Gradgrind.[8] Religion teachers will encourage pupils to remain open to what has been called 'a profound living knowledge of God.'[9] They will certainly want their pupils to be able to situate the historical Jesus in space and time ('fios'), and will also want them to grow in their understanding of his message ('eolas') so that they might perhaps come to know HIM who is alive and get to know him more and more each day. In short, when teaching pupils to be both knowledgeable and learned, teachers will live in hope that their pupils might also become wise.[10]

The enormous challenge of knowing God more clearly in Jesus Christ is therefore a major aspect of the Christian faith. This faith suggests a fascinating richness in God, a depth of mystery and of personality that would stretch the mind and imagination of any person. In the traditional Nicene Creed, our faith attempts to talk about God as father and creator ('We believe in one God, the Father, the almighty, maker of heaven and earth'), about God as son and saviour ('We believe in one Lord, Jesus Christ, the only Son of God ... For us men and for our salvation he came down from heaven'), and about God as spirit and life-giver ('We believe in the Holy Spirit,[11] the Lord, the giver of life'). Yet, somehow, it is the one God we are talking about, it is the one God we believe in. Nothing in our everyday experiences prepares us for such a shock. Or does it?[12] Unless we are open to being shocked and surprised we shall never succeed in knowing God more clearly. For God is shocking[13] and God is surprising. Nevertheless, the shock and surprise are ultimately pleasant ones. God is good news, not bad – news that uplifts us and never paralyses us, news that even heals our paralysis, as the Gospel story constantly reminds us.

This leaves open the question: How can one enter into the mystery so as to get to know God? You can never get to know someone really well unless the person allows it. She can put on many masks and keep you forever in the dark. But, if she removes these masks and lets you gaze into her eyes and deep into her soul, if she opens up to you and speaks her mind to you, then you may slowly get to know her. What the believer needs to do is to listen, to be alert, to be attentive and receptive. Then one may come to know God, for God has spoken and is still speaking his mind to people today. As the Nicene Creed reminds us, 'He has spoken through the prophets.' We believe that God has spoken a definitive Word in Jesus Christ and that this Word is still present and alive today. The task of believers is constantly to welcome that Word, to listen attentively to it, to reflect upon it and to try to fathom its richness and its challenging personal and communal implications. This is the surest means believers have of coming to know God more clearly.

However, there is no cheap grace. Coming to know God is bound to require time and hard work, as people make a continuous effort to penetrate God's word and grasp its fundamental meaning. Parents often underestimate how much help they can offer their children in this aspect of faith development. Children ask questions. They are constantly curious. A parent who engages with these questions in a welcoming way, who answers as truthfully as is possible for young minds to grasp, and who is honest enough to recognise a question for which there is no really satisfactory answer (Why did God make robbers?), is educating the young child to respect knowledge and its beauty and its limits. A parent who loves to tell good stories to a child is actually laying the firm foundations for that child's imagination to thrive in school and all through life. If, for want of parental encouragement, a child is not willing to ask awkward questions and not ready to trust her imagination, all subsequent learning of religion is sure to be boring or irrelevant. The exciting process of modern Irish primary school catechesis will become a daily chore.

Parishes too can contribute modestly to the intellectual nourishment of believers. Some people will be inspired by good homilies to go away and read the scriptures regularly and meditate on them. Others might join Bible study groups where they can share their insights and difficulties with others. There is scope too in parishes for book-circles to read works of theology and grow in awareness of the richness of the Catholic intellectual tradition. A parish newsletter or missalette can offer reflections on the Sunday readings or commentaries on the new Catechism. Courses can be arranged for liturgical readers or Eucharistic ministers to help them in their ministry to the parish. Parishes might even collaborate with local authority sponsored personal development courses by offering some spiritual input to enrich them yet further. Parishes might explore the world of local radio, with a view to making worthwhile religious programmes for the general population; they might alert any interested people to distance-learning facilities for adult religious education such as those on offer from Maryvale in Birmingham; in some cases a parish might even surf the Internet looking for stimulating theological or spiritual items.

In every situation mentioned above, the key requirement for intellectual growth and deeper knowledge and understanding of the faith, will be a certain openness of heart. God, indeed, has already suggested the importance of being open, by giving people two ears for every single mouth. These two ears should help all believers in 'the gradual grasping of the whole truth about the divine plan', and assist them also in 'the learning of tradition' (GCD, 24). As people develop their skills as religious thinkers, learn how to read the sacred scriptures with a critical eye and learn how to interpret the lessons of Church history, a new and exciting Church will be born. In this Church the whole community will become more careful, more knowledgeable, and more skilled in dealing with religion. In short, it will be a 'religiate'[14] body.

The desire to link what has been called 'personal knowledge' with 'factual and systematic knowledge' in such a way that people may have 'living knowledge of God' is a constant in the history of catechesis. When concrete narration was at the heart of catechesis, it was deemed important to be able to lay bare the highlights of salvation history in a schematic fashion. Telling the story of God's love for humanity with a view to evoking personal faith was important, but no less important was the construction of a system which revealed the meaning of this story. St Augustine talked of this system or schema or outline by using the image of a gold band which unites many diamonds in a chain.[15] That's why I refer from time to time to the Nicene Creed. Basically, of course, this is a liturgical prayer. It is a profession of personal and community faith. However, one cannot help noticing how it is also a schematic expression of the meaning of the Christian faith in a Triune God.

*Personal knowledge needs to be linked with factual and systematic knowledge.

Nicene Creed = ① is a liturgical prayer
② a profession of personal and community faith
③ a schematic expression of the meaning of the Christian faith in the Father, Son + Holy Spirit.

3

LOOKING AT LIFE THROUGH THE EYES OF CHRIST

See CCC 64, 218, 436, 702, 711-715, 904-7;
also TYMB 117-118

A person of faith is a worshipful person who is growing in knowledge of God day by day. Worship and knowledge of God will inevitably colour the way such a person views the world and life in general. This is the perspective of the General Catechetical Directory when it says that 'Catechesis has the task of ... teaching the faithful to give a Christian interpretation to human events, especially to the signs of the times' (26). What is being referred to here is the prophetic dimension of the faith. I am using the word 'prophet' in the original sense of 'someone who speaks on behalf of God' (God's mouthpiece or spokesperson). As the Nicene Creed states: 'He has spoken through the prophets'. The new Catechism refers to 'two prophetic lines...one leading to the expectation of the Messiah, the other pointing to the announcement of a new Spirit' (711).

The difficulty of the prophetic task is well known and well articulated in the scriptures. Moses felt unable to speak for God to Pharaoh, so much so that Aaron was drafted in as his mouthpiece (Ex 6:30). Jeremiah lamented his youth and offered this as an excuse for not wanting to become a prophet (Jr 1:6). Even Jesus, just before he summed up his prophetic ministry with the supreme prophetic gesture of going to a crucifying death, asked that the cup might pass him by. Prophets have traditionally been extremely unpopular. Like modern intellectuals, they are often regarded as cranks, because they speak the truth to those in power. Is it realistic to expect that people of faith will want to be prophetic? What does this mean, in the first place?

One way of understanding the work of prophets is to consider the concert pianist who has before her (physically, or in her memory) what non-musicians might regard as simply a series of lines and dots – the musical notation. By creatively interacting with that score, the musician interprets what the composer wrote, and through her playing enables the listeners to 'meet' the composer. The genius of the pianist lies in her mediating between composer and listener. This she does, not in a mechanical manner, but firstly through being a listener herself and secondly playing what she has heard. One might suggest that the prophet is God's concert pianist (this is just a minor shift in the basic image of mouthpiece).

The prophet mediates God's mind and will to God's people, not in a cold and routine way, but out of her own receptive openness to that mind and will. The prophet's 'musical score' is life in all its complexity. To this complex reality she must be very attentive. She must read, not lines and dots, but 'the signs of the times.' After creatively reading[1] the signs of the times, the prophet then expresses a unique vision to God's people. The prophet, therefore, is open to life, attentive to life, changed by life. She is someone who recognises God's call as it echoes through the circumstances of life and the daily encounters with the world and its peoples and institutions. The prophet is a generator of vision – God's vision. She interprets God's vision to God's people (CCC 64, 218). She helps them to see life as God sees it. President Mary Robinson's report on Somalia had a visionary or prophetic quality about it. So too did many of the Radharc programmes on issues of justice and peace in the world. It is sad to see the demise of such prophetic vision.

For Christians, Jesus is the supreme prophet (CCC 436). He is the one who supremely mediates God to God's people. Already we mentioned that in Baptism we are baptised into the priestly,

Immortal Diamond

kingly and prophetic ministries of Jesus. As maturing believers, we are meant to have the mind of Jesus, the vision of Jesus, to participate in 'Christ's prophetic office' (CCC 904-907). We are expected to see in life what he saw, to look at life through his eyes. One of St Paul's letters contains a plea that we have that mind in us 'which was also in Christ Jesus' (Ph 2:5-11). Though great, he opted for smallness. Though Lord, he became servant. What all of this suggests is something of the paradox of Jesus – his vision, his perspective, his viewing stance is a rather unusual one. As we try to look at life through his eyes, we are looking there for a greatness that is never too big to dirty its hands doing insignificant and menial tasks, like washing disciples' feet. We are looking out for a power and authority that serves and builds people up rather than one that crushes and oppresses them ('he will not crush the reed' – Isaiah). In short, we are turning upside-down and inside-out some of the normally accepted standards of the world. A prophet is bound to be perceived as a kind of a revolutionary.

A prophet *sees,*[2] *judges*[3] and *acts*. In the sense of Martin Luther King's 'dream', the prophet sees a vision and then judges in accordance with this vision: firstly, himself, then his Church, and then the world at large. He judges if the criteria, values and standards of Jesus are operative in these areas. Whenever a prophet sees true greatness of soul or true service of human beings, he will be to the fore in acclaiming it, encouraging it and fostering it. He will be, like Barnabas in the Acts of the Apostles, a true 'son of encouragement'. His approach will be that of the Beatitudes: 'Blessed are the …'. Like Jesus he will compliment people for the faith and goodness and generosity they show. He will suggest to them that they are the bright lights in God's vision of things.

On the other hand, the Christian prophet sometimes has to say 'Woe to you who are…'. When he looks at himself, his Church and his society and sees there pride, greed, abuse, the domination of the weak by the strong, the enslavement of the underdog by the powerful, he feels bound in conscience to expose these evils. Quietly, sincerely, he must call a spade a spade. With dignity and firmness, he must challenge people to ask the real questions. This is not idle chatter or mere words but *true action*. Good education should prepare people for this kind of noble action. In fact, 'the educator, ideally, seeks to encourage others to be seekers, always asking of social, political, economic and linguistic systems, "must they be this way?"'[4] It is encouraging to read in Frank McCourt's *Angela's Ashes* the role played by the primary school teacher, Mr O'Halloran, in giving McCourt a sense of prophetic indignation which allowed him to record in stark prose the poverty, exclusion and injustice suffered by him and his family fifty years ago in Limerick.

To approach life in this way – encouraging the good and exposing the evil – is to follow in the prophetic footsteps of Jesus Christ. It is to walk the lonely path of Jeremiah, who was called upon both to build up and to tear down. This double task has been highlighted as a requisite of the future Church. According to Rahner[5] only 'a socio-critical Church' will be a faithful Church. Such a Church will be actively prophetic. And it may expect that such action will provoke *reaction* – abuse, lack of understanding from others, accusations of faithlessness, prison, suffering, rejection, maybe even death. What sustains the prophet? Basically, it is the confidence that, because God raised Jesus from the dead, this same guarantee of resurrection is his. Having sealed his faithful people with the Spirit of Confirmation, God will not abandon his faithful prophets as they 'test and interpret all things in a wholly Christian Spirit' (*Gaudium et spes*, 62).

Prophets are often described as cranks, dreamers, or revolutionaries. It is normal for them to meet with much opposition. Why is this so? It is part of the ongoing struggle between the individual and the collective, between the new and the old. At the deepest level, all institutions fear the prophet. Bíonn an fhírinne searbh (the truth tastes bitter). The institutions everybody belongs to, such as family, Church and school, are by nature conservative. Their greatest strength lies in their ability to preserve tradition. They are structurally solid, while prophets are iconoclasts. In the context of a Christian family, it is not uncommon for children to challenge the religious lives of their parents. Children hate hypocrisy, and that is what makes them such powerful prophets. But the prophetic spirit they feel within can so easily be stifled unless parents are open to their hesitant critiques and ready to make some reasonable changes. If parents encourage the good, and lament the evil their children do, if parents act prophetically by building up and tearing down in the context of family life, then children can risk being prophets at home. One suspects that Jesus learnt some prophecy from Joseph and Mary.

And what about the parish? Can it foster prophecy? The answer must be a qualified yes. In many subtle ways parishioners can give life to the prophetic spirit. By taking care to study the work of the biblical prophets and by proclaiming their powerful words with clarity, passion and conviction during the Sunday liturgy, parish readers can inspire a parish to move beyond maintenance and strive towards mission. In many and varied ways the same process can continue through the weekly parish newsletter which, as well as giving local news, can also alert parishioners to God's vision of life. Where necessary a parish newsletter could, for example, call for ecological sensitivity. At any moment it could give a voice to the voiceless of the parish. In these and other ways the prophetic witness of the parish could be slowly incarnated.

One of the most interesting discoveries made by Martin Kennedy in his recent research into the provision of Adult Religious Education (ARE) at parish level in Ireland is that most adults are not interested in ready-made programmes.[6] They prefer to be given an opportunity to discuss the real live problems of their community and only then to begin to devise some manner of reflecting on these issues in the light of the Gospel vision of faith, hope and love. It would seem that the *sensus fidelium* is tending towards a prophetic stance. From this it seems reasonable to suggest that what parishes can best do is provide for the parishioners a form of ongoing, occasional ARE rather than inviting them to come and listen to programmes developed elsewhere.

All schools pride themselves on being depositories of traditional wisdom and received values. The educational logic of what has been said about the need for a prophetic spirit is that every school should be generous enough to allow for a questioning of the ordinary assumptions of school life. Many aspects of the school curriculum (e.g. the teaching of science and literature and history) ought to facilitate the growth of the pupil's critical abilities and thereby allow for real prophecy to occur. But there is another aspect of school life that should also be mentioned here, namely; the role of the artist in schools. Artists and prophets inhabit the same fragile world. They see what the rest of us barely notice. Therefore, in Catholic schools (both primary and second-level) there should be a genuine space for displaying good art and also a time for the celebration of Christian art. Nothing is better than art for generating vision, giving a sense of perspective, allowing for broad interpretation, and facilitating imagination. Here is an area of education where boards of management can come into their own. Recognising the intricate relation between school and leisure, they should see to it that schools are not held hostage to ideological or vocational gods, but rather liberated by art and its educational potential. At the limit, such boards may even need to fight for greater leisure within education.[7]

There are many different ways of teaching religion in school. The traditional catechism approach was very suited to an era in which people were not encouraged to ask too many questions. The catechism asked the questions for them and also offered them ready-made answers. Nowadays, in order to allow for greater participation and to sharpen pupils' critical faculties a number of interesting new approaches to teaching religion have been devised. Richard Reichert has outlined a simple teaching strategy in four parts.[8] For him, learning religion begins from the pupils' starting-point, evokes their significant experiences, facilitates reflection and makes space for assimilation. Thomas Groome's 'shared praxis' approach also allows for a critical education.[9] After naming present action, pupils are invited into critical reflection, and then, after hearing the Story and Vision of Christian tradition, they are allowed to dialogue with this as they speak their own story and articulate their own vision.

The Mater Dei Institute of Education has developed a meta-strategy called experience-tradition. Based loosely on Reichert's theory and more closely related to the work of Groome, it begins by evoking pupils' experience. After some initial reflection on this experience, there is a moment called 'voicing tradition'. In the light of personal experience and traditional experience, pupils can reflect critically on a particular topic and then plan some future action. The implicit anthropology in this meta-strategy is one that invites pupils to enter in to their own deep selves and speak truthfully out of these depths; it then asks them to stand back from their own private truth to listen to the voice of tradition. As they take in the values and critique the weaknesses of traditional wisdom they are thereby strengthened to go out into the larger world and move forward into a more just future. They are being apprenticed to a life of prophecy.

Though Ray Brady's *The Christian Way* series is no longer used in schools, it deserves special mention here for the brave effort it made to encourage prophetic pupils.[10] It sought to relate the adolescent experience of fault-finding and criticism with the religious experience of prophecy. The teacher's texts made a useful distinction between two types of criticism that are often levelled against religion. Religion can have critics from outside, who will suggest it is just a nuisance or even harmful. But the critics from inside will suggest that religion is not being faithful, that it is becoming false. Such were, for example, the Old Testament prophets like Amos, Hosea and Micah. They were 'critics from inside' who highlighted all that was false – the idolatry, the superstition, the hypocrisy, the legalism, the blindness, and the complacency.[11]

After second level, as people continue to mature in their faith they will need, among other things, to be educated for dissent.[12] Few people will be brave enough to take on a prophetic ministry within the Church. Few will be radical enough for such an undertaking. What if they were invited to consider the example of the great religious founders? In their own time these founders were usually dismissed as cranks and lunatics, but truth will out, and God's Spirit will find a way to speak. Through the prophetic voices of Benedict and Francis, Teresa and Mary Aikenhead, God's spirit was able to enliven the Church. The idea of creative dissent is, in fact, the fuel that fires the religious life in the Church. Members of religious orders have felt themselves called to burn so much with divine love that their whole lives are consumed in this flame.[13] The rest of us need to learn from them how to be prophets today.

We need to learn to be prophets today.

Eschatological Dimension:

4

BUILDING THE FUTURE IN HOPE

Associated with the theme of Hope.

See CCC 1042-50

Fascination with the future seems to be a constant part of human experience. Those who gaze into crystal balls can make a living by catering for this fascination. People are still prepared to pay money to hear others tell them what their future will be. They are so willing to read the advice of astrologers, that newspapers print horoscopes with a solemnity once accorded to Lenten pastorals. In all these cases the main interest seems to be to find out what **my** personal future will be. But it is also possible to want to know what **our** human future will be, or even what the **cosmic** future will be. The human lust for specific, detailed knowledge of the future of the world has generated great apocalyptic images in certain biblical books such as Daniel (7-11) and Revelation (8-22). In modern times there are many strange apocalyptic sects throughout the world, which claim that the world is about to end. Sometimes we hear of mass suicides by sect members, as in Switzerland recently where forty-six people were found dead.

However, in this context, it is worth recalling that neither Jesus nor Paul encouraged this tendency. They counselled, instead, a kind of agnosticism. 'Nobody knows the day nor the hour.' The future, according to them, remains ever hidden in God. However, since God is faithful to his promises, the future must ultimately be good. This knowledge should be enough to sustain us as we await in hope. Such was the attitude of many early believers, who prayed 'Come, Lord Jesus.' This attitude is not shared by everybody. When Alvin Toffler wrote *Future Shock* he suggested that the future was like a hostile force invading the present.[1] Those unable to cope with the invasion are like people

Building the Future in Hope

overcome by a foreign culture. They suffer, not from 'culture shock', but from 'future shock'. Toffler maintains that this illness can be fatal. To complicate matters further, at any time of high unemployment it is common for people to fear the future.

In short, there can be many different attitudes towards the future. We may wish to map out our personal journey through its hidden terrain. We may be curiously fascinated by its unpredictability. We may want to control it imaginatively. We may trust its basic goodness or fear its hidden threats.

Critics of the Christian faith have often been quick to point out the occasional naivety towards the future which some Christians have displayed. These critics accuse such believers of a quietism, a fatalism, a total acceptance of the future as inevitably a mere continuation of present inadequacies. They criticise believers who, according to them, want no more than 'pie in the sky when you die'. And these believers will often try to justify their position by pointing out that God's future, being gift, must be awaited patiently. It cannot, as it were, be forced out of God's hands. It cannot be shaped, they say, by merely human effort.

The question for many believers today is this: While recognising that the future is in God's hands, while recognising that the hidden future is ultimately God's gift to us, is it possible to remain inactive, waiting merely to be gifted, or is it not demanded that we answer the call to build a better future, such a call being implied in the very meaning of the gift on offer? What is the significance of the fact that the five wise virgins, while waiting for the arrival of the bridegroom, took care to have adequate supplies of oil for their lamps? A Christian attitude towards the future might well be summed up in the phrase 'While waiting, take care'.

With the publication of theological works[2] that emphasise the future dimension of faith, it is easy to want to contrast this forward-looking approach with the apparently backward-looking concerns with tradition. Hans Küng warns against this too-ready dichotomising of the time-structure of Christian faith. He points out, for example, that 'Jesus simply did not follow at all the line of the apocalyptic writers – who concentrated their whole interest on the future – but kept to the tradition of the great pre-exilic individual prophets who spoke at one and the same time of past, present and future.'[3] This is also the view of Thomas Groome, who describes Christian religious education as 'a political activity [any deliberate and structured intervention in people's lives which attempts to influence how they live their lives in society] with pilgrims in time that deliberately and intentionally attends with them to the activity of God in our present, to the Story of the Christian faith community, and to the Vision of God's kingdom, the seeds of which are already among us'.[4]

Indeed, such is also the movement of the Nicene Creed. It is in the context of belief in God, who sent a saving Son and raised him from the dead (story and its present realisation), that we express our conviction that 'his kingdom will have no end' and state our willingness to 'look for the resurrection of the dead'. Andrew Greeley[5] very subtly links the past with the future by suggesting that the traditional question 'Who **was** Jesus of Nazareth?' can be translated into present-day language as follows: 'Are there any grounds for **hope**?'

The rewriting of traditional formulas in the language of today is a constant feature of modern theology and religious education. Ever since Pope John XXIII reminded us of the fact that 'the substance of our faith is one thing, while the manner of its expression is another', there has been a willingness to undertake the onerous task of reformulating our traditional faith statements. The 'resurrection' spoken of in the Nicene Creed and often sung at Mass as if it were a past reality (when people wrongly say/sing 'He *has* risen'), can, in fact, be understood in a future perspective as well. Küng suggests that 'resurrection means to anticipate confidently the promised kingdom of freedom and to give people hope, strength and a will to serve so that death does not have the last word with us.'⁶ A similar point is made by Monika Hellwig, when she states that 'at its most fundamental what we have to hand on [tradition] is the experience of the promise that has totally transformed our perception of the world and of our life in it and the long experience of the community's response of faith and hope and action on the strength of that promise'.⁷

All of these authors are attempting to link past, present and future within the life of faith. They suggest the image of faith as the heart which feeds the eye (hope?), which sees the vision that the hands (love?) want to paint. Whether we emphasise the role of faith in moving people forward with a purpose,⁸ or the positive influence of future hope on faith today,⁹ or the Christocentric and cosmic dimensions of hope,¹⁰ in the last analysis, 'what Christianity needs are men who grounded in faith and animated by charity are willing to live a life of hope'.¹¹

There is no question here of being committed to building castles in the air or tilting at windmills or dreaming up utopias.¹² What is at stake is the belief that Christian faith involves a certain attitude of willingness to work for God's future, and for the coming of God's kingdom. This attitude can be expressed as follows: a person of Christian faith is someone who, listening to the past with critical charity, sees to the present with imagination, as he/she looks to the future in hope. In a paradoxical sense, one can even say that hope is the 'foundation of religious education'.¹³ Such a hope ensures that 'one lives a life of courage, vigour, confidence, commitment, and generosity. One never stops trying, never gives up, never sinks into a rut, never turns back, never refuses an opportunity to help, never rejects the possibility of reconciliation, never thinks that it is too late to begin again.'¹⁴ If one prefers a more socially oriented version of this description of hope, one could refer to what Küng once wrote: 'If I believe in an eternal life, then, in all modesty and all realism and without yielding to the terror of violent benefactors of the people, I can

Immortal Diamond

work for a better future, a better society, even a better Church, in peace, freedom and justice – and knowing that all this can only be sought and never fully realised by man.'[15] The idealism of this statement is tempered by a certain healthy realism which is also adverted to by another theologian, when he describes our best efforts to date in building a just world as no more than 'anticipatory incompletions'.[16]

When the General Catechetical Directory was written, its authors felt compelled to examine the relationship between faith and hope, between present involvement and the future eschatological fulfilment in Christ. This is how they expressed that relationship: 'Catechesis, therefore, performs the function of directing the hopes of men in the first place to the future goods which are in the heavenly Jerusalem. At the same time it calls men to be willing to co-operate in the undertakings of their neighbours and of the human race for the improvement of human society' (29). What is proposed here is a close link between hope and present involvement.

The sport of **beagling** could provide an image of this important link between hope/anticipation and present effort. In beagling, a pack of hounds chases after hares or foxes or stags. Once they get the scent they run off in pursuit. After them, on foot, come the beaglers – men, women, children of all shapes, sizes and levels of fitness – whose whole enjoyment consists of taking part in the chase. No animal is ever caught. Hounds and humans pursue the animal without ever reaching it. The hunted animal beckons forward. It generates the chase. But the chase is its own justification, its own reward. As Gratiano says in *The Merchant of Venice*, 'All things that are, are with more spirit chased than enjoyed.' Such, in a sense, is the life of faith. One is always moving forward in pursuit of an ideal which can never be fully realised, the partial realisation of which both satisfies and yet calls anew.

Beagling is very much a minority interest in Ireland. Its

influence is minimal. Not so our literature. Many of the influential writers who have treated of the after-life in novels, poems and plays, have offered our imaginations very gloomy images indeed.[17] We have the atmosphere of fear and terror in Bram Stoker's *Dracula*, where the un-dead wreak havoc on the living and threaten to condemn them all to a vampire existence of living death. Samuel Beckett's *Waiting for Godot* has been interpreted as a parody on Christian hope. Waiting for the second coming of Christ is compared to the eternal waiting for a non-arriving Godot. Hope is flawed because it is absurd to wait like this. Flann O'Brien's strange world, as portrayed in *The Third Policeman*, is one of humour, certainly, but even more so of riveting bleakness, where everything bad in the here and now is even colder and more imprisoning in the hereafter. Everlasting life is profoundly monotonous. Derek Mahon the poet introduces us to an eternal life that is not matched with eternal youth. It is en endless cycle of reincarnation, each phase totally other than the preceding one, wherein it is possible to become a cricket. Such negative images of after-life that occur in many modern Irish authors provide a powerful cultural challenge for Irish believers. Against these modern literary images of the afterlife, Christian faith offers the stories of the risen Lord Jesus appearing to his frightened disciples and bringing peace, reconciliation and courageous hope. One wonders which kind of image of eternal life is uppermost in the consciousness of modern Irish people. There is clearly much catechetical work to be done to present the eschatological focus of Christian faith in a way that is ennobling, enriching and life-giving for all.

Priests in parishes can provide a catechesis of hope by introducing God's people to the lives of all the great saints. When celebrating saints' feast-days, the very least they should do is give some background information about them. But this is not enough. Since saints are proposed to believers for their admiration and to encourage their life of faith, hope and love, it is imperative that the real saints and not their plaster images be put before God's people. As real believers who met great challenges and came through trials and tragedy with God's grace, saints are clearly people who can inspire deep hope in us. That is why we need a thorough familiarity with them and need to hear their life stories told over and over again.

Christianity has given the world many men and women who have been shaped by their living Christian faith and, in turn, have shaped their own times and ours: *missioners* such as Paul of Tarsus, Patrick, Cyril and Methodius, Francis Xavier, Damien the Leper; *martyrs* such as Irenaeus, Polycarp, Agnes, Cecilia, Thomas More, Paul Miki and his companions, Maximilian Kolbe; *bishops* such as John Chrysostom, Athanasius, Gregory the Great, Hildebrand, Thomas à Becket, Lawrence O'Toole, Charles Borromeo, Francis de Sales, John XXIII; *theologians* such as Augustine of Hippo, John Damascene, Bernard, Thomas Aquinas, Alphonsus Liguori; *monks and mystics* such as Antony the Hermit, Benedict and Scholastica, Columba and Brigid, Hildegard of Bingen, Catherine of Siena, Julian of Norwich, Teresa of Avila, John of the Cross, Thérèse of Lisieux; *friars and reformers* such as Francis of Assisi, Dominic, Ignatius of Loyola; *outstanding women* such as Mary mother of Jesus, Monica, Margaret of Scotland, Clare, Bridget of Sweden, Joan of Arc, Margaret Mary Alacoque, Nano Nagle, Mother Teresa; *teachers* such as Cyril of Jerusalem, Bede, Anselm, John Baptist de la Salle, Edmund Rice, John Bosco; *lovers of the poor* such as Wenceslaus, Vincent de Paul. To learn the story of their lives is to undertake an apprenticeship in hope.[18]

We live in a very violent age. In a world where news worthiness is identical with disaster and where we are so often exposed to images of death and destruction, we are all in danger of being submerged in a flood of despair. People lament that there is little good news in the news broadcasts. Is there anything we can do to minimise such a deluge of negativity? Yes! And it is quite simple. Every faithful person today should let loose a parallel flood of images. We could, for example, keep a diary of hope-filled experiences, jotting down each day a list of hopeful stories as we encounter them. We ought never reply to the problems of evil by simply constructing a rational argument for the goodness of God. Sad people cannot be reassured out of despair. There is only one valid response to the prophets of gloom and that is to insist on telling them modern stories of hope. We long for the day when the *seanchaí* tradition of Irish folk culture will be resurrected and people of faith will become more involved in local newsletters, local radio and the national press, precisely to tell these startling stories of hope.

Stories of child sexual abuse have been some of the saddest stories to be told in modern Ireland. Even incest has been brought out into the full glare of the media. When parents sexually abuse their own children, it is hard to remain calm. This is quite unfortunate, given that the majority of parents truly love their children and do for them only what is best. A powerful example of the positive influence parents can have on their children is provided day after day by the manner in which most parents deal with the failures and failings of their children. When children do wrong, or fail to live up to agreed standards, a good parent will not explode into rage but will wait in patience for the chance to encourage a fresh beginning. Children who have done wrong or failed to do good need to know that they have not thereby forfeited the love of their parents. When this becomes clear to them from the forgiveness offered by their parents, then they are no longer prisoners of their failures but free to be their better selves in the future. It is in ways like this that the foundation of Christian hope is laid down in the hearts of young believers.

When death strikes, it is hard to sustain hope. Why did God take her away? How can we survive without his support? Irish traditions of waking the dead and attending funeral services are central to developing in our community a deep sense of hope. Hence the responsibility that devolves upon parish teams to prepare and celebrate vibrant funeral liturgies. Hardly anything else in the life of the average parish does more for fostering communal hope. Within a culture of faith-inspired communal hope, it is relatively easy to offer further grounds for hope at weddings, Easter Vigils, Pentecost ceremonies of light, and Christmas.

It is common to hear the question today, how can schools best foster hope? The first reply must be to point out the role of the school ethos in this challenging task. If the school treasures academic excellence and also works hard for the least able pupils; if the school fosters all the talents of all the pupils, and discovers the talents of those who appear to have none; if the school is unambiguous about the standards of behaviour and relationships expected of staff and students but is also willing to forgive the offenders and the recidivists; in short, if the school has a truly Christian ethos, then everybody in the school community can begin to grow in hope. At the level of formal classroom teaching too, the school can raise the profound questions of evil and of human destiny and explore these from a Christian perspective. For example, an English textbook for early secondary school touches on the theme of hope during the summer term of second year.[19] Topic 4 is entitled 'What does the future promise?' This aims at showing that the future builds on the past and the present; at reflecting on the phrase in Ecclesiastes that 'there is a time for everything'; and at seeing what are the hopes and ambitions of the Christian. There is a long list of New Testament references which deal with such hopes and ambitions. Topic 6 tries to show that hope is one of the strongest human forces. It explores some features of the virtue of Christian hope and looks at some prayers of hope. These are drawn, not just from the scriptures, but also from some well-known spiritual writers.

Irish religion textbooks have reflected much on the theme of

Christian hope. It would be hard to better the following definition of hope: 'True hope rests in God's abiding presence with us in his Holy Spirit. We believe the Spirit will continue to bestow his gifts on us, despite our waywardness. We believe he will ultimately direct man and his world towards the fullness of life – something we must wait for with patience'.[20] We should be glad to see the extent to which such themes are dealt with in many of the modern religion textbooks in use in Ireland.[21]

5

CHANGING RADICALLY UNDER THE SPIRIT'S INSPIRATION

See CCC 1427-33; 1700; 1877; 1965-74; 2050-55; also *TYMB*, 115

This aspect of mature faith is referred to as follows in the General Catechetical Directory: 'Catechesis performs the function of disposing men to receive the action of the Holy Spirit and to deepen their conversion. It does this through the word, to which are joined the witness of life and prayer' (22). Implicit in this phrase is the notion that the moral life of believers is based on a profound change of values called *conversion* and that the agent of this conversion is none other than God's Holy Spirit. People of faith can be described as those who are open, as Mary was, to the influence of this Holy Spirit. They are growing in receptivity to the Spirit's action within their lives. They listen to the Spirit who speaks through the scriptures and his mouthpieces the prophets, and who also addresses them in silent prayer. Since their listening is a serious one, they cannot remain unmoved or unaffected. In responding they are inevitably changed. They become a new creation.

Moral theologians refer to this process as 'call and response' or, sometimes, 'gift and call'. Enda McDonagh refers to morality as 'man's response to God'.[1] God is the mystery who communicates himself to people. To those who are open to God's Spirit, to those who try to listen to the Word of God, God is experienced as a two-edged sword. God cuts people open and exposes both their greatness and their misery. God reveals people's greatness, in so far as he affirms their likeness to himself, their being made in his image. God also unveils people's misery, since he accuses them of always failing to measure up to that image. In short, God reveals to them that they are at once beloved children of God and miserable sinners.

The liturgy of Ash Wednesday reveals very well this paradox at the heart of faith. As they take the ashes, believers are invited to turn back to God,[2] to make a U-turn on the road of sinfulness and come back home immediately. It tells them that 'now' is the acceptable time. The word 'now' could suggest 'merely now, but not any other time'. However, in the context of repeated Lents, 'now' can only mean a 'continuous now'. In other words, it is *always* necessary to turn back, to make a fresh start, to initiate a new beginning. The direction of the change called conversion is clearly 'towards God' and the timing of this change is 'always'. For it takes time and patience to develop attitudes of openness, conversion[3] and renewal. The creation of a new human being in the image of the Son of God requires much patience from the potter God and much reworking and reshaping of the human pot. It takes a lifetime to work out and actualise 'the moral requirements of religion and the religious requirements of morality'.[4]

Conversion cannot be a change that touches merely the fringes of our life, or something that engages us only at a superficial level. God's word, his two-edged sword, pierces our persons right through to where our inner core is situated. God's two-edged sword is meant to cut out the very roots of our sinfulness and not just to lop off the rotten leaves that flutter in full view. The reason why this section has been entitled 'changing radically' is to try to highlight the nature of the change that is involved in conversion. *'Radix'* means 'root'. That's where God wants to change us by his word, since that's where our attitudes and our prejudices are formed. That's where our personality grows and develops, where our values are fashioned and our treasure is stored. The new Catechism treats many of these themes, e.g. human dignity (1700), transformation (1877), new law (1965-74), and becoming perfect (2050-55).

Changing at this deep level is called *metanoia,* repentance or conversion (CCC 1427-33). It involves turning away from sin and turning back to God. The Christian way of life, the life of faith, is nothing other than a constant conversion. It is a long drawn out struggle along the road of life. Realising that we are motoring in the wrong direction, we try to slip from fourth gear into second, then watch for a break in the oncoming traffic, then swing the car around with much screeching of brakes, then try to coax it back into third, and then into fourth and, maybe, for some people, even into overdrive.

In every celebration of the sacrament of Baptism, the water, the candle and the christening robes remind us that a radical change is taking place, that a new birth is happening before our eyes. Though the Nicene Creed hints at this newness, when it states that 'we acknowledge one baptism for the forgiveness of sins', in our ordinary experience we seldom witness the really startling nature of baptismal change. Perhaps, if we had more adult baptisms in the future, we could renew the old tradition of baptism by immersion. The adults would undress, cast off their old clothes, walk down into the baptismal pool, then step out on the other side to be clothed in fresh white garments. They would be seen to be 'putting on Christ', turning over a new leaf, becoming a new creation. That's what baptism is about, since that's what faith is about. It's a matter of the new replacing the old, of leaving the past behind and boldly stepping into God's future.

The Nicene Creed functions as a statement of our identity as believers. In it we solemnly proclaim that 'We believe in ... God the Father ... in one Lord, Jesus Christ ... in the Holy Spirit ... in one, holy, Catholic and apostolic Church.' This means that we are conscious of being children of God, of being Christ-people, of being Spirit-people, of being Church-people. We have many ways of answering the fundamental question, 'Who am I?' Sometimes it can come as a surprise to us when, listening to the first Eucharistic Prayer, we hear that Abraham is called our father in faith.[5] At first, is seems strange that someone who called God 'El' rather than 'Abba', who predated Jesus Christ by over a thousand years, who knew no Pentecost nor Apostolic Church, should be proposed to us as our father in faith, as our faith-model. However, on reflection, it is easy to see the wisdom of this proposal.

For Abraham allowed the unknown God to enter into his life. And, as a result of being so open, Abraham was never the same again. After meeting God, it was God's promise that made sense of all Abraham's plans and commitments. In response to God's gracious promise, Abram (as he used to be called) changed his name to Abraham. He thus became a new person, a new creation. He left his home and relatives behind and set out into the unknown, hoping gradually to find what God was promising him. In this sense, the whole life of Abraham sums up beautifully what it means to change radically in response to God's word, God's Spirit, God's call, God's promise.

We, who admire the faith of Abraham, begin to understand how such faith is a divine gift[6] which we are meant to receive both freely and actively. Faith is our response to God's Holy Spirit, who blows where he wills throughout the world. As the General Catechetical Directory reminds us, catechesis is concerned with 'disposing people to receive the action of the Holy Spirit and to deepen their conversion'(22). Abraham's story, Abraham's pilgrimage of faith is the paradigm for our journey of faith. In his life we are confronted with the very structure of a faithful life. Above all else, such a life is made possible by God's promise of a brighter future. This promise then converts us into people of thankful response.

The dialogical structure of the life of faith is wonderfully conveyed in the early chapters of the Acts of the Apostles. There we read about the preaching of Peter and how he claimed that, in raising Jesus from the dead, God was proving himself absolutely faithful to his constant promises. We read there also of the response made by the people who heard this kerygma. It was simple. They wanted to know 'what must we do?' And Peter invited them to turn away from their sins and be baptised. Having heard the good news, they were meant to be converted. Having been promised God's gracious gift in Jesus Christ, they were to regard themselves as called to worship God through, with and in Christ.

In much the same way, too, Mark's Gospel presents the whole teaching ministry of Jesus. Jesus' teaching is, firstly, a proclamation of the presence of God's kingdom in the world. And, secondly, it is a challenge to all people to respond to this offer by being converted and by committing themselves to the values of this kingdom. Conversion, in the sense of a radical change for the sake of God's promised kingdom, is of the essence of a life of faith.

We all long for stability. We are all conservative at heart. We tend to favour the status quo. We are loath to change, especially when the change required of us is profound and demanding. This universal experience of human beings is challenged constantly in the Eucharist.[7] Here we have a celebration of the dramatic change and transformation that took place in the death and resurrection of Jesus Christ. Here we have the pledge of Jesus' Spirit, who is the very source of new life, the Spirit who changes us into images of Jesus Christ. Every time we celebrate Mass in a spirit of faith we admit our desire for and our need of conversion. In fact, the very first joint activity at the beginning of Mass is called the Penitential Rite. Here we admit that we need to change for the better and, in confidence, we ask God to make this possible.

Furthermore, when we approach the sacrament of reconciliation,[8] what we are doing is thanking God for the forgiveness offered us in his Son, rejoicing because we have often been uplifted in the past through receiving this forgiveness, admitting that we have not always been as faithful to God as God has been to us and pleading for the strength to change now into more faithful followers of Jesus Christ. In short, whenever we celebrate these two sacraments of radical change (Eucharist and Penance), we hear God calling on us to step out of the darkness into the light, out of chaos into life, out of our own security into God's better future.

What God expects of us and what our faith requires is that we leave our comforts and our past behind us, in order to step confidently like Abraham into the unknown future. This was well appreciated by Pope John XXIII. In his last hours (24 May 1963) he wrote the following: 'It is not that the gospel has changed: it is that we have begun to understand it better. Those who have lived as long as I have ... were enabled to compare different cultures and traditions, and know that the moment has come to discern the signs of the times, to seize the opportunity and to look far ahead.' Looking faithfully and confidently to the future means that, at a personal level, one hopes for personal renewal and conversion.

But there is more to faith than this, since, as believers, we are not just solitary individuals. Together we create many structures, many institutions, and these, too, are in need of constant renewal, reformation, *aggiornamento*. A book outlining the educational role of the parish pointed our that 'the job which parishes should be structured for is the work of fostering conversions to Jesus within the Christian community'.[9] In other words, the very *raison d'être* of the institutional reality of the Church (whether it be sacramental ritual, parish structure or the like) is to make conversion possible for believers. Within this perspective, it is eminently sensible to want to change our structures as soon as we recognise that they are hindering rather than favouring the conversion process of the people of God. Structural as well as personal change must be part of the believer's radical conversion. This theme will be examined in more detail under the heading of the socio-political dimension of the faith.

Let us return to the paragraph from the General Catechetical Directory quoted at the beginning of this section. There we saw that catechesis performs three related functions in leading believers to radical change. These are called word, witness and prayer. Let us now consider these three, but in reverse order. Central to moral catechesis is *prayer*. The relevance of the catechist's or teacher's prayer to the process of conversion consists in this, that prayer highlights very clearly the inner dynamic of faith. In prayer, one listens to and allows oneself to be changed in response to God's Spirit. For a believer, faithful prayer is a form of radical change.

Secondly, *witness*. This is crucial in trying to identify the role of parents in the moral education of their children. Parents may or may not be able to explain the origins of their moral values, they may or may not be able to discuss complex moral issues with their children, but one thing parents can always do is live their moral values. By witnessing to courage, honesty, fair play and tolerance in the family environment, parents make it possible for their children to learn these values by a process of osmosis. Children, in fact, will normally imitate their parents' values. Not of course the merely professed values, but the really lived values. Example serves where precept fails. Children can sense the moral depths of their parents and children hate hypocrisy. Children learn moral values in somewhat the same way as they learn to speak their native tongue, by listening, observing and imitating.

A similar process takes place wherever young people are socialised, in the neighbourhood or the local parish or the school. Whatever values are truly operative in these environments will be taken on board by young children in an intuitive and unreflective way. The school ethos is a potent carrier of moral values. Long before the child is taught in class to reflect on moral issues and reason about moral values, the child will already have learnt to be moral in a particular way from merely going to school and being exposed daily to the school ethos. The mission statement of schools often lists the implicit values by which the whole school is trying to live. Hopefully the whole school, management, administration, teaching staff and pupils, will live these values each day. This is the greatest possible help the school can give to the moral development of its pupils. As well as this, it is very important for the teacher in class to be open to questions, comments, critiques from pupils and to be ready even to modify teaching plans in response to pupils' real needs. As Pope Paul VI reminds us, 'modern man listens more willingly to witnesses than to teachers, and if he does listen to teachers, it is because they are witnesses'.[10]

And, finally, *word*. Another aspect of the school's contribution to the moral development of pupils is the provision of good, critical religious education. This kind of religious education will explain the basic attitudes of openness and conversion which are at the heart of faith. But it will not be limited to giving explanations. It will also encourage pupils to be prophetic and ask why the world is the way it is. In seeking to find worthwhile answers to this fundamental question, critical religious education will offer pupils the wisdom of their religious tradition. It will do this in a respectful way, always acknowledging the central value of pupils' freedom. It will avoid all forms of religious indoctrination but will try, instead, to expose the subtle forms of indoctrination that modern secular culture often indulges in. For example, the myth of human progress, the myth of 'West is best', the myth of 'might is right', the myth of 'God is dead' or the myth that 'science knows all'. Brenda Watson's justification for religious education in schools is that critical religious education actually allows pupils to detect the real but hidden indoctrination of spurious values to which they are daily exposed, or the even more sinister omission from education of the spiritual aspects of human experience. 'Indoctrination works by sending the mind effectively to sleep, so that what is impressed upon it is soaked up as by blotting paper.'[11]

Much valuable moral education takes place through liturgical homilies. The sermon in James Joyce's *Portrait* conveyed a sense of terror as the key motive for a moral life. 'Hell is a strait and dark and foul-smelling prison, an abode of demons and lost souls, filled with fire and smoke.'[12] Though there are clear echoes here of the warnings given by Jesus concerning the fires of Gehenna, it is doubtful if this sermon accurately reflects the thrust of Jesus' message of good news. The motive of terror is not central to the moral teaching of Jesus. What one finds at the heart of his moral teaching is rather the startling gospel of love: if God has loved us so passionately, then we should love God, love each other, love ourselves, and love the world. In good homilies believers are reminded of God's great love so that they are empowered to change to a new way of living, to a new set of values based on God's love. The task of the homilist each Sunday in a parish is to pour out on the gathered believers a constant drip-drop of divine compassion, so that their hearts of stone may be worn down by God's word and converted into hearts of flesh. This is moral education for people of faith.

Good moral preaching is much more than just saying what's in the commandments. People already know what's there. What they are more likely to need is words of encouragement. They need to be reminded time and again that moral living is possible, given God's love, given God's grace. 'What God commands he makes possible by his grace' (CCC 2082). A similar dynamic can also occur in school. Moral teaching in the classroom is not simply telling pupils what's right and wrong: anyone, even a computer, can tell that. A good teacher, however, is able to do much more than simply explain what Christian morality means in a particular case. The good teacher of morality has great story-telling ability. In the Christian and Jewish religious traditions, the moral life begins in careful listening to the greatest love story ever told, and leads on to recounting all the subsequent versions of it in the lives of good-living people. A painstaking analysis of this 'careful listening' and regular story-telling can deepen moral insight and strengthen moral discernment. This is not a job for solitary individuals. Moral education is a communal activity. Teachers of morality should be able to conduct a good discussion. One of the strengths of the original *Christian Way* series was Ray Brady's treatment of moral values in the Christian life. Throughout his textbooks the following words can be noted – *appreciation, sensitivity, openness.* Obviously these are attitudes to be encouraged in pupils because they have a moral significance. It is clear that faith and morality go hand in glove. In fact, so closely are they related that one entire textbook is largely concerned with cultivating the moral dimension of the faith.[13] Its central chapter (6) explores the Sermon on the Mount, and presents this as a challenge to believers to change their attitudes and values radically. Some of the practical applications of this key chapter are worked out in detail in chapter 3, where pupils are alerted to the moral issues involved in urban poverty, unemployment, pollution, war etc. These are areas in which profound changes are required if life is to be humanly liveable. Chapters 8-11 are also moral in tone. They deal with some of the moral values that derive from the sacredness of life, from the mystery of human love and the work of justice.

In this section we have been looking at faith as a process of radical conversion in response to God's word. This concept is at the base of another popular religion textbook that deals specifically with moral education within the context of Christian faith.[14] It sets out to identify the many agents a believer needs to listen to and to be open to in the attempt to form a Christian conscience. The key to this book is called the STOP-SIGN, a technique which invites the pupils to Search out the facts, to Think of alternatives and consequences, to consider the effects on Others (and to consult them) and to Pray. Surrounding the STOP-SIGN is a list of persons, realities and institutions that need to be listened to: Jesus, Reason and Revelation,

Imagination, Law, Church, Values and Instinct. Finally, one listens to one's CONSCIENCE. All of these realities are, though in different ways, 'the voice of God' – a voice calling for radical change.

In school, it is not only the religion teacher who engages in moral education. Religious and moral questions can surface during the teaching of any subject in the curriculum.[15] An obvious example is when a biology teacher discusses issues of genetics, or a geography teacher raises issues of population control, and human fertility, or an economics teacher explains the mechanics of debt in the developing world. The teaching of literature, whether drama or poetry or the novel, regularly leads to serious moral discourse. A school production of a medieval morality play or Shakespeare's *Macbeth* or Anouilh's *Antigone* can help to sensitise the moral antennae of pupils. A study of well written articles in the daily press could do wonders for the moral education of young people today.[16] Nuala O'Faoláin laments that 'there seems to be no desire to speak about the faith, or if there is a desire, no language to use'.[17] One of the major tasks of education in religion must surely be to make pupils religiously literate.

6

BUILDING COMMUNITY

CCC 2401-2442; 2302-2317

The General Catechetical Directory states that the worship aspect of faith cannot be divorced from the socio-political.[1] It expresses well the union of these two aspects, when it maintains that a person mature in the faith 'is impelled to communion with God and with his brothers' (23). Having already explored the worship dimension ('communion with God'), we turn now to explore the theme *'communion with his brothers'*. The God we believe in is a community or communion of persons – a community so united that it is one. The Spanish writer Juan Arias has suggested that one of the reasons we find it so hard to come to terms with the Blessed Trinity is simply this: we never experience any human community so united in its members that it really is one. Since we have no experience of such a human community, we naturally find it difficult to develop an analogy from community when thinking about God.[2] Arias' comment suggests the following reflection – maybe we should be actively involved in trying to build real communities wherever we are. This work of building community might deepen our appreciation of the Blessed Trinity. And then, as we grow in knowledge of this central mystery of our faith, the Triune God would offer us a paradigm for all human community development.[3]

The Nicene Creed challenges our faith when it asserts that 'we believe in ONE, Holy, Catholic and Apostolic Church'. We are all conscious of the disunity that exists among the followers of Christ. Even within the Roman Catholic Church there is often a tendency to polarise and to separate into neat little divisions.

There needs to be much give and take between conservatives and progressives if such potential divisions are not to develop even further. A person of mature faith, conscious of this tendency, would always see him/herself as a bridge-builder, or even as a fire-prevention officer, when friction tends to ignite the flames of passion and engulf the Church in a roaring fire of bitterness and recrimination. The prayer of Jesus was 'that they all may be one as thou, Father, in me and I in thee'.[4] In other words, God's oneness is made. It is a given. However, we have to make our human oneness. We have to build community, in order to become one. Our faith in the one God is understood here as a dynamism that helps people to carry out their 'human responsibilities and the duty of solidarity' (*GCD,* par. 23).

We are reminded by the Nicene Creed that God is the 'creator of all that is.' From this it follows that we need to be committed to working for unity, not just among ourselves (within the Church), but also within society; and also to working for the well-being of the entire physical world. God is, of course, profoundly interested in the well-being of human beings. 'God wills nothing but man's advantage, man's true greatness and his ultimate dignity. This then is God's will: man's well-being … at all levels … the salvation of man and of men.'[5] As Dermot Lane puts it, 'The God of the Kingdom is always a God who is for the individual.'[6] Every time we pray the Our Father and say 'Thy will be done', we are pledging ourselves to collaborating with God in bringing about people's well-being.[7] However, we are coming to see more clearly every day now that the Christian God is Lord, not just of the Church and of human beings but also of the whole cosmos. In virtue of their faith, Christians should be passionately committed to fostering ecological well-being. This newly-discovered ecological significance of Christianity suggests the image of faith as a work of art or an artistic faith celebrating and sustaining God's total creation.[8]

In recent years, many encyclicals have urged a world-wide

perspective upon us. Examples would be *Pacem in terris* and *Populorum progressio,* both of which are concerned with the global issues of peace and human development, and which draw much inspiration from Vatican II's *Gaudium et spes.* The South American liberation theology movement has also taken up these themes. Pope John Paul II, in his travels throughout the world, has regularly encouraged the local Churches in their attempts to help build a peaceful, just community whenever violence, injustice and lack of unity prevail.

There are still some faith-people who feel that such emphases are an aberration, and a departure from the traditional faith. They feel uneasy when theologians write about 'A kingdom of Justice, Peace and Love'.[9] To such people perhaps the following lines of the Psalm 82 can be a challenge.

> God has taken his place in the divine council;
> in the midst of the Gods he holds judgement:
> How long will you judge unjustly and show partiality to the wicked?

Vatican II's final document was entitled *Gaudium et spes* or 'The Pastoral Constitution on the Church in the Modern World'. A careful analysis of this document suggests the following pen-picture of the modern believer: **The believer has a serious responsibility, greater even than that of other human beings, effectively to work with all people of good will for the justice that leads to unity – and to do this in the light of the hoped-for kingdom.** What I propose to do now is to comment on this pen-picture, within the context of faith coming to full maturity.

The *seriousness* of the human responsibility for a more just and more united world is stressed in *Gaudium et spes,* as follows. As befits its generally open perspective, this document states that the 'monumental effort of mankind through the centuries to improve the circumstances of the world, presents no problem to believers: considered in itself, it corresponds to the plan of God' (34). The human race, as God's image and likeness, is meant to bring order out of chaos, to bring light into darkness, to bring life where there is none. Human beings are called to be creative. By filling the earth and bringing it under careful control (in the imagery of Genesis), humans are most true to themselves.[11] They are most authentic in being creative. Their daily work can be seen 'as a prolongation of the work of the creator.'[12] Because of many complex historical factors 'the human family is gradually coming to recognise itself and constitute itself as one single community over the whole earth'.[13] There is now a new sense of the creative potential of the human race[14] being activated through various agencies of international co-operation. This potential, however, is seldom realised because of war and greed and economic recession. 'With an increase in human power comes a broadening of responsibility on the part of individuals and communities.'[15] Believers, as part of the human family, have therefore a serious responsibility for building up the world.

Responsibility for building up the world, for building community, for working towards a just and peaceful world is a responsibility shared by the whole human family. However, *Gaudium et spes* strongly suggests that, in virtue of their faith, Christians have an *even greater responsibility* than others. Of them to whom much is given (faith is the supreme gift), much more will be expected. 'Hope in a life to come does not take away from the importance of the duties of this life on earth but rather adds to it by giving new motives for fulfilling these duties.'[16] 'It is a mistake to think that, because we have here no lasting city but seek the city which is to come, we are entitled to shirk our earthly responsibilities; this is to forget that by our faith we are bound all the more to fulfil these responsibilities according to the vocation of each one.'[17]

People who were once used to hearing about the believer's duty to 'renounce the world' may be somewhat taken aback to read paragraphs such as these. However, there is a way of linking these apparently novel perspectives with the more traditional one of renunciation. A modern theologian suggests that 'to work creatively to change or transform it is precisely what it meant by renouncing the world'.[18] Faith has the task of renouncing, not so much the world in itself, as any tendency to absolutise the world as we find it. This is the perspective of mystics such as Meister Eckhart. We have already come across this notion, when considering the believer as a visionary and prophet. As such, the believer will always be relatively uncomfortable within a world that still has much improving to do. His kingdom-oriented faith will be building up within him a sense of unease at the present inadequate realisations of justice, peace and unity. The believer will be aware that 'God's Heaven refers man to the earth ... from the hope of God's future the world (and its history) is to be differently interpreted and consequently decisively changed.'[19]

That it why the Irish Bishops appealed to their flock to ask themselves whether their 'concept of religion gives proper place to justice and charity as well as to Mass and the sacraments and prayer. If it does not, then it could not claim to be the religion of the Bible or of Jesus Christ.'[20] These are strong words, suggesting as they do the seriousness of linking justice and faith in an integrated life style. There is a powerful echo here of Vatican II's request: 'Let there, then, be no such pernicious opposition between professional and social activity on the one hand and religious life on the other.'[21]

Gaudium et spes stresses the importance of believers making an *effective commitment* to building up a better world.[22] A benign interest in worldly affairs is not considered to be enough. The believer ideally would be immersed in them. There would be no room for a 'hurler on the ditch' attitude. 'In their pilgrimage to the heavenly city, Christians are to seek and relish the things that are above; this involves not a lesser, but rather a greater commitment to working with all men towards the establishment of a world that is more human.'[23] This is probably the key quotation of our analysis. It links up with what I have already said about responsibility (here called 'commitment'), and also about faith binding us all the more (here called 'greater commitment'). Furthermore, it anticipates what still remains to be said about the context and the purpose of the work of justice – the cosmic and unitive dimensions are expressed here by the phrases 'with all men' and 'more human world'. It also points to kingdom-hope as the motivating force of this commitment.

For the moment, however, I merely want to emphasise the 'work' element, the activity, the doing, the praxis. We are reminded here of the scriptural advice to 'strive to enter by the narrow door' (Lk 13:24). Striving, here, is part of the imagery of an athletic contest. Indeed, the recent phenomenon of the Dublin City Marathon can assist our reflections, since it conjures up images of many different people responding at many different levels of commitment to the same race. Those who go to look at the runners and shout encouragement and offer them sweets and drinks are at one level of commitment. Those who train enough in order to finish, are at another level. Those who train to win, are at another. But all are 'working', all are in different ways 'effectively committed'[24] to the race and are totally different from those who merely view it on TV or read about it in the newspapers.

The ecumenical or universal dimension of the believer's responsibility for the world's advancement in expressed in the following manner: 'The Council ... exhorts Christians to cooperate with all in securing a peace based on justice[25] and charity and in promoting the means necessary to attain it, under the help of Christ, author of peace' (*Gaudium et spes,* 77). 'Although the Church altogether rejects Atheism, she nevertheless sincerely proclaims that all men, those who believe as well as those who do not, should help to establish right order in the world where all live together. This certainly cannot be done without a dialogue that is sincere and prudent' (21). One senses in these two quotations a genuine effort, on the part of the Council fathers, to open up the Church in the direction of collaboration with people of good will, the establishment of a kind of Rainbow Coalition. After centuries of quoting the Master to the effect that 'he who is not with me is against me', they now desire to make sense of that other statement of the Master, where he says that 'he who is not against us is for us'.

Taking these two paragraphs (77, 21) together also gives us an idea of what the overall purpose or goal of the dialogue is meant to be. Whether one calls it 'securing a peace[26] based on justice and charity' (77) or the establishment of 'right order in this world' (21), it is really the same goal as outlined in the key paragraph 57, namely, 'a world that is more human'. When paragraph 92 treats of the 'dialogue between all men' it summarises all these ideas, as follows: the Church has the 'mission to enlighten the whole world with the message of the gospel and gather together *in one spirit* all men of every nation, race and culture...'. In short, all the efforts undertaken by believers (in dialogue with others) at building a better world are ultimately concerned with the final prayer of Jesus 'that they all may be *one* as thou, Father, in me and I in thee'.

What force or dynamism could propel believers along the paths of unity, peace and justice? The answer to this question is hinted at in many places throughout *Gaudium et spes:* it is nothing other than the eschatological dimension of our faith, the *hope* we have of God's coming kingdom. This hope is the very impetus which ought to carry believers forward in their commitment to justice in the world. If Christian hope was ever a justification for inactivity in the face of injustice, it should now be the very pulse and heartbeat of our involvement in the work of justice. 'There is no question, then of the Christian message inhibiting men from building up the world or making them disinterested in the good of their fellows: on the contrary, it is an incentive to do these very things' (34). 'Far from diminishing our concern to develop this earth, the expectancy of a new earth should spur us on, for it is here that the body of a new human family grows, foreshadowing in some way the age which is to come' (39). Given what has been said above about the need to collaborate with people of good will, even with non-believers, in the task of bringing about a more just world, it seems that the difference between believers and non-believers is not to be found in their search for justice, for this in fact can actually unite them. Perhaps the difference is to be found in the very Christian hope which inspires the believers and which is not part of the experience of the non-believers, whose attitude is usually one of 'a loyalty to the present life, to the earth as sole fatherland, refusal of any suggestion of consolation in the hereafter.'[27]

Parish is ideally the pre-eminent place for catechesis. In regard to the socio-political dimension of faith, the average parish can achieve a great deal. An obvious contribution would be the provision of special Lenten liturgies using the material offered by Trócaire on social justice issues. The time of Lenten fasting and almsgiving could then become a time for assuming our Christian responsibilities for the poor in our world, and for learning something of the meaning of mercy (trócaire) in the life of faith. At any time during the year a parish could organise a liturgy for its own sick people. In bringing the sick and housebound to the parish church and in laying hands on them to heal them, the parish could discover in a powerfully symbolic way that its real purpose is to reach out and minister to all those who are in any need. Parallel with these special liturgies there could well be a series of homilies from time to time, outlining the bases for a spirituality of justice work. Any parishioners engaged in this kind of work would be greatly empowered if they were helped to see the clear connection between the faith they profess and their work for justice. In particular, homilists ought regularly to encourage politicians and all those in public life to take seriously the challenge of creating a more just, more peaceful and more united world.

Of all the aspects of mature faith, the socio-political dimension probably emerges most forcefully and thrives most readily in the life of adults. The complexity of social issues makes this dimension of faith more accessible to people of greater experience. But experience is not enough by itself. People also need help to make sense of that experience, before they can link it to the life of faith. One thing that could be done for adult believers would be to teach them the skills of social analysis. If a single parish could not rise to this, perhaps a group of parishes could combine. But perhaps an even better way to do this would be to see if such social analysis was already being taught within general adult education and then to link the interested parishioners with this enterprise.

The adult focus of the socio-political dimension of faith does not mean that children should be blocked from exploring it. Schools can help in cultivating a spirit of social justice throughout the believing community by sowing the seeds of justice awareness among the very young. One of the most exciting developments in recent years in primary schools is that when children are learning respect for God they also learn respect for God's world, for each other, and for themselves. They are taught to take responsibility for the school premises and the local environment. A school ethos based on justice for all and a parental ethos of fair play in the family are corner-stones in the construction of a child's sense of justice.

Second-level religion textbooks have been enriched in recent years by the inclusion of many social justice issues. The textbooks often assume that a dichotomy can exist in the experience of young believers between their search for personal salvation and their desire for the improvement of the world. Being more introspective than extrovert at the time of adolescence, they need to be encouraged to look beyond their own immediate personal problems to the larger issues of the world. The poet, Henry van Dyke, expresses this teenage dilemma very well, when he writes:

> Who seeks for heaven alone to save his soul,
> May keep the path, but will not reach the goal;
> While he who walks in love may wander far,
> But God will bring him where the Blessed are.[28]

To save one's soul one must be open to saving the world. For that reason, the teenagers are invited to consider 'our collective responsibility for waste, discrimination, injustice', or even to 'consider work as a human issue in today's world'.[29] When more and more people have no jobs to go to, it is not correct to talk merely of a markets problem or of the need for political intervention. In a world of increasing unemployment, the obvious economic and political problems can mask an even more profound spiritual crisis. For how can those with no work assume their God-given responsibility towards a better world? This kind of justice education, however, should never be allowed to generate a culture of despair among young people. They are not responsible for the mess the world is in. They will have to do something about it. But perhaps not yet. In the meantime they should learn about the great contribution made by the Christian faith tradition to the betterment of the world. They could be introduced to the work of Crosscare, St Vincent de Paul, Concern and Goal. They could be taught about the history of hospitals, schools, universities and monasteries in Christian lands.[30]

Many of the modern religion textbooks are not happy simply to present information about the work for justice and peace. They also encourage pupils to go beyond the stage of mere analysis and understanding to the praxis stage of taking a stance and doing something in terms of the knowledge already acquired.[31] A good example of this approach can be found in the following Action Project: 'As a group, devise some project that will do two things: (1) Let your stand on the pro-life issue be known (for example, by writing letters to newspapers, legislators etc.); (2) Raise money to help an organisation like Birthright. Perhaps the fund-raising can be organised in a way to let people know why you are raising the money.'[32] The use of the word 'why' makes this Action Project much more than simply social work. Since it springs from faith reflection and attempts to justify itself, it also has an educational dimension. It is, in fact, learning through praxis. When examining the presentation of faith and justice issues in second-level religion textbooks, it is important to distinguish clearly between pupils' work for peace and justice and the work of adult citizens and politicians in this area.

The wide variety of imaginative approaches to linking faith and justice is to be lauded.[33] There is one drawback, however. So much good work has been done in recent years in this area of faith education that an interesting point has now been reached. Some at least of the graduates of Ireland's schools say that they have received far too much of this content when learning religion at school. Maybe we have been too successful. Now that students have got too much of this, we need to remember that 'they are as sick that surfeit with too much as they that starve with nothing'.[34]

7

WORKING FOR CHRISTIAN UNITY

CCC 817-822

Just beside 'The Young Traveller', a hostel for young people off Dorset Street in Dublin, there is a building referred to locally as The Black Church. This building is not a Catholic church. In the north-city folklore children learn that if you run around this church twice, you will see the devil. Here we have a classic example of anti-Protestant feeling, communicated in the form of a ritual taboo. The memory of such prejudice is still vivid to many Dubliners and could, no doubt, be matched by many similar memories from other parts of Ireland and from across the religious divides. The Protestant church in Doon, Co. Limerick, was known to local Catholics as the 'preaching church', and its weather vane was called the devil. Obviously, ecumenism needs to be high on the list of priorities for all believers in Ireland. And this, of course, poses problems for catechists and religion teachers – how can people be educated in the faith in such a way as to make ecumenical dialogue a reality in their lives?

When *Catechesi tradendae* was published in 1979, it included a few paragraphs on the ecumenical dimension of catechesis.[1] It stated that 'catechesis cannot remain aloof from this ecumenical dimension, since all the faithful are called to share, according to their capacity and place in the Church, in the movement towards unity.'[2] An awareness of the difficulties encountered twenty years earlier by Pope John XXIII, when he was trying to establish the Secretariat for Christian Unity just before Vatican II, suggests that we have come a long way as a Church since then. To hear the present Pope maintaining that ecumenism must be on the faith agenda of *all believers* is quite a change from the earlier attitude in Rome, that ecumenism was an optional extra for a few eccentrics on the fringe of Church affairs. Nevertheless, it is one thing to write an agenda; it is quite another thing to carry it out. The 'Black Church' mentality is still with us and needs to be overcome if ecumenism is to thrive.[3]

Many theologians assert that faith itself grows and matures only when it has an ecumenical or *outreach* dimension. 'The faith of Irish Catholics is incomplete and impaired in so far as it does not recognise the divine revelation coming to them through the people, practices and traditions of other Irish Churches.... The non-Episcopal churches, for example, with their greater awareness of the priesthood of the whole people and of all as full and, so, equal members of the Church provide an obvious source of theological enlightenment and practical guidance for the hierarchical Churches with their temptation to first and second class membership and to confining initiative, responsibility and authority to the upper levels of bishops and clergy.'[4]

Already in 1971 the General Catechetical Directory, had outlined the ecumenical goal as one of the *long-term goals* of catechesis. Catechesis should assist in restoring the unity of Christians as follows (27):

(a) 'by clearly explaining the Church's doctrine in its entirety.'

(b) 'by fostering a suitable knowledge of other confessions, both in matters where they agree with the Catholic faith and also in matters where they differ.'[5]

(c) 'it should avoid words and methods of explaining doctrine that could lead separated brethren or anyone else into error regarding the true doctrine of the Church'.

In regard to (a) above, which mentions the need clearly to explain the entirety of Church teaching, much has already been said in our earlier analysis that could prove helpful here, specifically, the emphasis placed on being able to present the faith in a systematic manner through relating its many aspects to the Paschal Mystery which lies at its core. It could be said that the entirety of Christian faith and the entirety of Christian doctrine is, in fact, the crucified Jesus who is now the risen Christ. To the extent that the believer is able to relate every part of the faith-edifice to this corner-stone, he or she is well-prepared for ecumenism.

Such a believer will be able to distinguish what is central to faith from what is peripheral, and what is essential from what is passing. Such a believer will realise how all the individual mysteries of the faith are linked to the central mystery of Jesus Christ, and how all these mysteries can be clearly understood only if seen in the light of the mystery of Jesus Christ. Such a believer will recognise the Trinity in the Father's anointing of his Son, Jesus Christ, with the Holy Spirit; she will see Incarnation in the Son becoming man; she will understand Redemption as Jesus, the liberating saviour, saving people from sin and evil; she will think of judgment in terms of Jesus Christ the eschatological judge; and she will rejoice in the forgiveness of sins as God's *'hesed'* made flesh in Jesus Christ. What we are hinting at here is called the organic character of the content of catechesis (GCD 39). In other words, there is a certain harmony between the various aspects of the faith. There is a certain interrelationship of themes. To appreciate this is crucial for clearly explaining the entirety of Church teaching. Obviously, therefore, it is also crucial for advancing the work of Christian unity.

This kind of ecumenical work is not for the faint-hearted. It makes great intellectual demands on its participants. It requires an ability to explain one's own Christian tradition in an honest manner and without shirking from controversial issues. From this it follows that, whenever Catholic pastors or catechists or religion teachers are being educated in the faith in seminaries or teacher education centres, they should be helped to value a systematic grasp of their whole tradition and to become aware of the historical development of all Christian doctrines.

An excellent methodology for this kind of fundamental theological formation is implicit in a recent book on medical ethics called *Life and Morality*. In it the author, David Smith, examines the issues of abortion, genetic engineering, in-vitro fertilisation and euthanasia. What is striking about the book is that the author, a Catholic theologian, presents a whole range of nuanced positions on these moral topics that have been proposed by the various Christian denominations. The precise position of the Catholic Church is clearly articulated and is shown to agree in some respects with, and differ in other respects from the position of other Churches. The ecumenical activity of Catholic Christians should flow from a deep appreciation of and rich understanding of the Catholic tradition and its varied teachings, within the context of the greater Christian world. 'Ecumenism presupposes denominational identity as a point of departure on the way to Christian unity.'[6]

The General Catechetical Directory also mentions *other criteria* which need to be taken into account when trying to present and clearly explain Church doctrine in its entirety. There is need for a gradual approach in the presentation, and for a suitable pedagogy in presenting the entire content (38). Furthermore, while acknowledging the Christocentrism of catechesis, the Directory also speaks of the Trinitarian theocentrism of the faith, and cautions that 'if catechesis lacks these three elements (viz. through Christ, to the Father, in the Spirit) or neglects their close relationship, the Christian message can certainly lose its proper character' (41).[7] Another perspective never to be lost sight of when trying to present the entirety of the faith is the salvation quality of our faith. 'To view the diverse Christian truths in their relation to the ultimate end of man is one of the conditions needed for a most fruitful understanding of them' (42). We are reminded here very forcefully of the fourth- century instruction of Cyril of Jerusalem which, in explaining the names of Christ, stressed how 'the saviour comes in various forms to each man for his profit.'[8]

Apart from these criteria the following points should be stressed when explaining Christian doctrine. Firstly, all doctrines of the faith are historical in character (44); and, secondly, 'on all levels catechesis should take account of the hierarchy of the truths of faith' (43). The importance of this last point is well expressed in the introduction to a modern 'essential catechism'. The author explains why he says 'nothing on the much controverted subject of papal infallibility. The reason for this omission is not that I reject the doctrine but that, despite all the controversy which has raged around it during the last hundred years, it is not at the absolute centre of the Catholic tradition. The Church was able to survive without its explicit formulation for eighteen centuries, and while infallibility may be important, it is not nearly as important as resurrection.'[9]

In regard to (b) above, the implications for catechists and religion teachers would seem to be that they need to be very aware of the basic similarities as well as the differences between the various Christian denominations. The very openness towards God, which we saw earlier to be the hallmark of the true believer, must express itself in openness also towards believers in other Churches. 'In Ireland today it is not possible to be truly Church without as Catholic opening to the heritage, life and aspirations of the Protestant Churches or as Protestant without begin equally open to the Catholic.'[10] In reality, however, the effort at being open is often complicated by the fact that during recent years much study and many agreed statements have given the impression that the Churches have much more in common than used to be thought in the past.[11]

The problem is further complicated by the fact that many Christian believers are now more at home with theological and devotional books written by Christians of other denominations than they are, at times, with corresponding works written by some of their own. Rahner and Barclay, to name but two, have succeeded in crossing the denominational barriers with much success. There is the real possibility that the great Christian divisions of the future may well transcend the existing Church boundaries. If the very success of ecumenical dialogue is not to create novel divisions where as yet there are none, then what is needed in catechists and religion teachers is an openness of heart and a passion for the truth, no matter on whose lips it is formed, no matter in whose lives it is lived out. The very same honesty that admits how much Christians have in common will also advert to the issues on which we still differ. That very same honesty will enable us 'to walk together,' as Alan Falconer puts it in his account of the Lima Report on Baptism, Eucharist, Ministry.[12] Then we shall be able to 'share more of what we have in common with one another – the saving power of Christ, for example, and the unity we have in our common baptism'.[13] We shall be able to rejoice together in the words of the Nicene Creed: '*One*, Holy, Catholic and Apostolic Church'.

A major task for all those who educate young people in the faith is to foster in them a healthy ecumenical outlook. This can be done by parents even with very young children. Above all else parents should treasure all their children equally. In spite of their children's differences in temperament, intelligence or personality, parents ought to treat them all as equally beautiful flowers in the family garden. This ongoing experience of diversity and equality can help even very young children to grow in respect for human differences and in toleration of human variety. Brothers and sisters regularly fight and argue with one another. In serious matters they can even become estranged. A parent who works to reconcile her bickering children, and encourages them to overcome division, is conveying to children an ecumenical spirit and providing a good basis for later ecumenical work.

Ireland will need an explosion of such ecumenically-minded families, if we are ever going to emulate South Africa and establish something like the Truth and Reconciliation Commission, wherein people can remember the ancient injustices in order to heal the memories, In the meantime, people can at least join together in various symbolic activities such as the annual Maracycle between Dublin and Belfast. It may not be much to cycle two hundred miles across Ireland with people of all denominations and of none. It generates only a limited sponsorship income for the charitable work of Co-operation North. But symbolic gestures of this kind can have a cumulative effect on a people. They are like the millions of drops of calcified water that coagulate into a stalactite and over a long time build a bridge between the roof and the floor of the dark cave of hostility.

How can the normal parish fulfil its catechetical role in regard to fostering ecumenism? First of all, the parishioners should be helped on an ongoing basis to see that ecumenism is not just a way of overcoming hostility and building bridges between the Churches. Ecumenism certainly has an ecclesiastical side to it. But at a deeper level, ecumenism also has a cosmic relevance. Jesus prayed that his followers would all be one 'so that the world may believe'. In other words, the very existence of faith in God throughout the world depends to a large degree on the example of unity among all Christian disciples. To believe this would be a inspiration for local ecumenical endeavour. Secondly, parishioners need to be shown that, as a body of Christian disciples in a world of many other Christian bodies, they actually need one another and cannot live as Christians without one another. To organise charitable bodies or educational provisions in an inter-denominational manner, to engage in joint pastoral planning with neighbouring denominations, to join in the Sunday services of other Christian traditions are, among the many practical suggestions for ecumenical enterprise that are offered in a fine article recently penned by Padraig McCarthy.[14]

Schools, too, can provide an ethos that fosters ecumenical openness. For example, catechetical programmes, both at primary and second-level schools, usually contain ecumenical material of a worship dimension. Liturgies and prayer services for Christian unity are timed to coincide with the week of prayer for Church unity which occurs in parishes every January. As Western Christians try to learn more about their Eastern sisters and brothers, it is gratifying to see in many second-level religion textbooks the very sympathetic treatment that is given to two of the treasures of Orthodox Christianity in order both to study them and to offer them for the enrichment of Catholics – these treasures are the *prayer of the heart* and the use of *icons* in worship.

Since lack of knowledge often leads to lack of love, it is good to see the effort being made in second-level religion textbooks to open the minds of young people to the wonders of other religious traditions. A 'Did you know?' twenty questions type of quiz, rich in information about other Christian traditions, can make ecumenical study more playful. Young people can be intellectually and emotionally stretched by their teachers who are willing to invite into their classroom guest speakers from other denominations, to arrange visits by their pupils to other places of Christian worship, and then to allow pupils to report on such visits, noting the similarities and differences.

One of the recommendations of *The Religious Dimension of Education in a Catholic School* is that religion teachers should be willing to collaborate with teachers of other subjects whenever religious themes arise naturally in those subjects (64). The teaching of European history is bound to raise some religious questions. History teachers confronted with the Great Schism of 1054 or the Reformation in the sixteenth century could well benefit from some cross-discipline contact with religion teachers. Historical knowledge of the division between Roman Catholics and Orthodox should extend beyond the dispute over the word *'filioque'* in the Nicene Creed. It could well include such liturgical issues as whether leavened or unleavened bread should be used at Mass, such disciplinary matters as clerical celibacy and whether clerics should wear beards, and of course, the whole question of the role of the Pope in the Universal Church. These are examples of issues that have both historical and religious overtones, and could hardly be studied without some co-operation among teaching staffs. The use of maps in such teaching also points to the possibility of cross-curricular work with teachers of geography.

In regard to (c) above, the background to this directive seems to be that for a long time there has been a tendency both in theology and in catechesis[15] to formulate Christian doctrine in a negative or defensive manner. Common examples would be statements such as the following: Catholics don't believe in abortion or euthanasia or divorce; Catholics don't believe in the private interpretation of the scriptures; Catholics don't believe that Jesus is merely a superstar. These belief-statements have been formulated mainly as opposition-ideas to heretical or erroneous notions. The effect on believers of over-exposure to such a way of expressing the faith is that they are often more likely to know what they *don't* believe in than what they do. This can leave the believers with a rather narrow, impoverished view of the faith. Then, as they attempt to express their faith to others, they can (often unintentionally) give to others a less than adequate view of what they believe in.

One way of attempting to minimise this problem is to try when possible to be more positive in formulating the faith. Such a positive statement of faith will be better suited to giving others an account of the hope that is within us. It should reveal rather than distort this hope. A colleague once suggested to me an example of the more positive approach to formulating the faith – instead of merely learning off the largely negative Ten Commandments, she encouraged her class to move towards the following statement: 'Put God at the centre of your life. Care for all those who cared for you. Leave every man his life, his wife, his good name and his property.' This is not a replacement for the Ten Commandments, merely a more positive way of expressing them.

8

SHARING FAITH WITH ALL PEOPLE

CCC 849-856

The General Catechetical Directory invites catechists 'to help these communities to spread the light of the Gospel and to establish a fruitful dialogue with men and cultures that are not Christian, preserving here religious freedom correctly understood' (28). If faith is to grow, deepen and mature then believers have to risk sharing it with outsiders. The idea of 'keeping the faith', in the sense of keeping it to oneself and trying to avoid contact with non-believers (for fear of contamination), is at least questioned, if not critiqued here. The perspective of *faith as outreach*[1] towards non-Christians, implies the Gospel notion that in giving we receive; that in sharing faith with others we can grow in our own faith; that in evangelising others we can, to some extent, be evangelised by them. Implicit in this notion of sharing is the notion that faith can be offered, but never imposed. The Crusaders misunderstood the nature of faith, not perhaps in its content, but certainly with regard to the dynamics of its growth.

The Council Fathers of Vatican II, speaking about what are often called the 'foreign missions', had this to say: 'The Church strictly forbids forcing anyone to embrace the faith, or alluring or enticing people by unworthy techniques.'[2] This statement reflects the idea of faith as a free commitment to God in Jesus Christ, and is concerned very much with the dynamics of coming to faith within the context of sharing, freedom and dialogue, honesty and truth. The movement implicit in faith as outreach is a very demanding and time-consuming and potentially dangerous one because it seeks to walk 'in the footsteps of Paul' the great evangeliser who was rejected, stoned, lashed, shipwrecked, jailed and finally crucified. He it was who believed that Jesus Christ had died once and for all and who formulated the vision of faith in terms of bringing all things together as one in Christ. Such a vision is still far from realisation. But it is precisely this vision that finds expression in our traditional Nicene Creed where we state our belief that it was 'for us men' (i.e. for all people) and 'for our salvation' that Jesus pitched his tent among us. His coming was for the salvation of all people. He is to judge 'the living and the dead' (i.e. literally everyone). It is within this universal, inclusive perspective that we must try to see our faith as a 'light to the nations'. We belong to 'one, holy, CATHOLIC (i.e. UNIVERSAL or INCLUSIVE), and apostolic Church.'

For many centuries Christian theology has taught that outside the Church (*'extra ecclesiam*') there is no salvation. A narrow interpretation of this aphorism would suggest that unless one were a baptised member of the (Roman Catholic) Church, one could not be saved. An equally narrow interpretation would condemn all those who did not belong to the (Orthodox) Church to the danger of perdition. Protestant interpreters of the same phrase have often stated that Roman Catholics are *'extra ecclesiam'* and thus on the road to hell. Clearly, if God's salvific will is for all people to be saved, then we must find some way of interpreting the phrase *'extra ecclesiam'* in a much broader fashion than has been customary. One way of doing this is to recall that, at its heart, *'ecclesia'* is 'God's convocation or gathering-in of people'. It suggests a divine calling, an offer of divine salvation and a human, communal response accepting that wonderful, unbelievable offer. It would follow from this interpretation of the phrase *'extra ecclesiam'* that only those who have heard the call of God, and then refuse to follow it by joining together in some community of faith, are in danger of missing out on God's salvation.

In any dialogue, there must be talking and listening, giving and receiving. The same pattern applies to every dialogue of faith. Earlier, in talking of the knowledge dimension of Christian faith, I emphasised the role of listening to God's word so that we can grow in an understanding of the faith. But then I spoke only of God's word in Scripture. We know, however, that God speaks his word to us in many other ways too. Today we are conscious that God addresses a saving word to his faithful people even from outside the narrow confines of our Christian faith. Vatican II talks of the 'seeds of the Gospel' existing in the great world religions and even in the hearts of good-living pagans and atheists.[3] If we take this idea seriously, then it must be the case that God is at work through the spirit of the risen Christ in these 'outsiders', in a manner we don't fully understand, but truly none the less. And, if God is really at work in them, then we can be evangelised by them. Our faith can grow through openness to God alive and at work in them. I would go even further and suggest that, as Christians learn to become open to the 'others' in their world, they will discover they are growing also in openness to God the Great Other in their midst.

In short, precisely as believers in God, we ought to be open to and actively 'listening to' other religions and ideologies.[4] This is the essential quality of faith as outreach. The purpose of this outreach is so that we can learn to recognise the 'seeds of the gospel' contained in them, e.g.

- the rich *humanism* of many atheists and agnostics;
- the Hindu concern for the sacredness of all *life;*
- the Buddhist *spirituality;* and
- the *submission* to God (the single-mindedness) of Islam.

After all, if Jesus (the object of our faith) is confessed by us as *truly human* (like us in all things but sin), if we acknowledge him to be 'the way, the truth and the *life*', if we remember him as a man of prayer and deep *spirituality* and if one of our central precepts as Christians is *obedience* to the will of the Father, then we do in fact share many basic values with these other religions and ideologies. As we learn to see these values incarnated outside the visible Church, we can be challenged as to the quality of their incarnation within our own believing communities.

Let us consider the situation of Muslim believers in Ireland today. Given that Islam is the world's third greatest monotheistic religion; and given also the growth of the Islamic community in Ireland in recent years (it is now larger than the Jewish community) it is altogether fitting that Irish people should be alerted to the religious values that are dear to all faithful Muslims and that govern their daily living. Islam literally means surrender to the will of God. This surrender or obedient submission is expressed in the five pillars of Islam, namely, Creed, Prayer, Fasting, Almsgiving and Pilgrimage. Muslims believe in one, merciful, almighty God whom they name Allah and to whom they pray five times daily. Ramadan is their month of fasting, not unlike the Christian Lent of old. Almsgiving recognises the link between religion and justice. Mecca is the goal of Islamic pilgrimages. Islam is a religion of the book. Their sacred scripture is called Koran, which literally means 'that which is to be read'. As believing Christians, we can learn much from Islam – specifically, avoidance of idolatry in the worship of a transcendent God; reverence for God's word; and the need for regular prayer and fasting. We can also concur with and possibly even share in their search for a greater justice in the world as well as echo their sentiment about being a pilgrim people on earth.

Of course, the learning is not meant to be all one-way. Just as we can learn from those outside the Christian faith, so too we can offer them a lot. Because we are grounded in a vision of Jesus raised from the dead, we can offer outsiders a firm conviction that all the human and religious values that we share together and that we all work so hard in different ways to nourish and develop, do in fact have a guaranteed future. Since they are in the hands of God, their future is to be transformed, purified and glorified by God in his Kingdom. And, because their ultimate future is guaranteed, they merit our care and support here and now in the present.

Parents who live a deep faith automatically convey the shape and structure, the tone and feel and firmness of that faith to their children. Thus they enable the children to put down strong faith roots, and to experience the stability and strength of faith in God. But parents also have another role to play in the development of their children's faith. They must deliberately help their children, not just to be firm and strong, but also to remain open to other faiths as well. And they can best achieve that objective by daring to introduce their children to new worlds, both cultural and religious. While young children need to be protected from exposure to too much variety so that they can grow into their own native tradition and feel at home in it, this should never be done through encouraging their incipient chauvinism. Our own language and traditions are worth treasuring, but not if we must despise any other language or traditions to do so. Our own is not the only valid way of being human and living humanly. Our own Christian faith is not the only valid way of being faithful in God's world. Lessons such as these are learned best of all in the family environment.

Priests in their homilies can continue this work of opening out minds and hearts which otherwise might close in and freeze. Following the clear example of the Lord, Jesus, whose Good News they are called upon to proclaim day in and day out, they themselves should be glad to be shocked by the level of faith that is often found in the most unexpected places. If Jesus could rejoice in the faith of the pagan Syro-Phoenician woman and the pagan Roman centurion in Capernaum, then preachers today should be bold enough to alert God's people today to the incredible reserves of genuine faith in the heart of today's pagan and secular world. In this context too, especially when preaching about Patrick or Brigid or Colmcille, priests have a great opportunity to highlight the fact that these early Christian missionaries in Ireland recognised much that was positive in the old Celtic pagan religion. There has been a wonderful awakening of interest in Celtic spirituality in recent years. As well as learning to practise that spirituality, it is good for the Irish person today to study in detail the Celtic religion of our forebears, in order to recognise, as Patrick did, its great spiritual riches.

As children move through primary school and are introduced to the pillars of their Christian faith, it should be made clear to them that all the great early figures of Christian faith belonged to the Jewish community of faith. Jesus was a Jew. Mary and Joseph, Peter and Paul were Jews. No aspect of Christian prayer life or ritual celebration can be adequately understood without grasping the Jewish roots of Christian faith. All Christian children should be taught to respect their Jewish roots and to treasure their Jewish cousins of today. While studying the creation stories, while reading about the Last Supper, and while praying the psalms, young Christians should grow to love not just their own Christian faith but also the Jewish faith of their ancestors.

In recent years many religion teachers have taken upon themselves the onerous task of introducing junior cycle children to the great world religions. Two particular approaches to this difficult topic should be noted. One is the encouragement given to teenagers to visit local synagogues and mosques, to experience the strangeness there and to reflect on the experience. The other approach is the inclusion in some text books of interviews with representatives of other religions. In both these approaches one senses a taking off of shoes and a reverence for the other religious traditions.[5] The ordinary Irish Christian man or woman would be surprised to learn of the range of other religions that exist in Ireland today. A recently published book gives a mine of information regarding the Jewish, Baha'i, Muslim, Hindu, Chinese, Buddhist and Sikh communities in Ireland.[6] Though

Sharing Faith with all People

the author was pleased to find out that these other religions have not experienced much hostility from mainstream Irish life, he was nevertheless saddened to discover the depth of Irish ignorance about these religions. One small and inexpensive way to banish some of this ignorance would be to publish and distribute inter-faith calendars which list all the great feast-days of all the great world religions.

The encouragement of greater openness between religious-minded people is not simply an issue for religion. Since all people of all religions and of none form part of the body politic, fostering their peaceful co-existence and mutual respect is clearly also a social and political matter. One way of doing this would be for the state to become more active in lessening religious tensions by publicising religious reconciliation and co-operation. The Government-sponsored TV service could contribute its own educational input by commissioning good religious programming dealing with the great world religions. The focus in such programmes need not be evangelical or missionary. All that would be needed would be a thorough social and historical approach. Programmes could examine the reasons why religious differences often keep tensions alive (e.g. in Bosnia, Algeria and Northern Ireland). They could also convey an account of how true religion can contribute significantly to peace-making. An example would be the manner in which Muslims have control of the Christian church of the Holy Sepulchre in Jerusalem in order to keep the peace between the rival Christian communities. Another example would be the manner in which Muslims respected so much the prayer life of Christian monks in Abu Ghosh, near Jerusalem, that they felt obliged to protect this Christian monastery of the East from attack by Western Christians during the First Crusade.

So far, we have talked about faith as outreach towards non-Christians. We have explored the so-called 'foreign missions', the people and cultures that are not Christian. In our analysis we have seen that many parallel values exist in these cultures. When we turn our attention to cultures that are called Christian (e.g. European or Irish cultures) we sometimes find alive in their midst many elements that are manifestly unchristian: violence, injustice, chauvinism, pride, materialism. All of these non-values need to be challenged by people of faith. There needs to be a constant evangelisation even within nominally Christian cultures. During the Second World War French theologians recognised this fact very forcefully when they referred to France as a 'mission-land'. Many modern thinkers would go so far as to suggest that Europe would best be called 'post-Christian' rather than Christian. It is this perspective which inspired the call of Pope John Paul II for a new evangelisation in Europe. The difficulties implicit in this task should not be underestimated. It is often more difficult to speak of Christ to those who have heard of him but have forgotten him or rejected him than it is to speak his words to those who have never heard them.

In the light of this idea of cultures that are not fully Christian (and what culture ever is?) what Pope Paul VI wrote in *Evangelii nuntiandi* begins to make sense. There, in paragraphs 70, 71, 72, he spoke of 'the laity', 'the family' and 'the youth' as agents of evangelisation, delineating the special field of each. Since lay people live in the vast and complicated worlds of politics and economics, since they are in charge of the world of culture, of the sciences, of the arts, of international life, of the media – it is here, in this 'culture', that they are to be evangelisers. This means that their faith will inspire them to identify, encourage and support every Christian and evangelical possibility which, though latent, is already present and active in the affairs of the world.

Then there is the notion of a micro-culture, e.g. the family. In this context, *Evangelii nuntiandi* talks of 'all the members evangelising and being evangelised. The parents not only communicate the Gospel to their children, but from their children they can themselves receive the same Gospel as deeply lived by them' (71). It is the experience of many pastoral workers that the persistent religious questions put by children to parents can often attract those parents anew to the religious quest. But the family milieu is not simply a place within which the Gospel is shared and transmitted. It can even become a centre from which the Gospel radiates. Here we have the notion of the 'domestic Church' – a potential evangeliser of other families in the immediate neighbourhood.

Evangelii nuntiandi talks about the role of young people in handing on the faith, especially within the so-called 'youth culture'. 'Young people who are well trained in faith and prayer must become more and more the apostles of youth. The Church counts greatly on their contribution, and we ourselves have often manifested our full confidence in them (72).'

TEXT-BOOKS CONSULTED

Aotearoa/New Zealand Catholic Bishops' Conference, *Understanding Faith* series (Auckland: National Centre for Religious Studies, 1991):
- UF3A- UF3H (PB)   Eight text-books for 13-14-year-olds.
- UF3A- UF3H (TB)   Corresponding teacher guides.
- UF4A- UF4H (PB)   Eight text-books for 14-15-year-olds.
- UF4A- UF4H (TB)   Corresponding teacher guides.
- UF5A- UF5F (PB)   Six text-books for 15-16-year-olds.
- UF5A- UF5F (TB)   Corresponding teacher guides.
- UF6A- UF6H (PB)   Eight text-books for 16-17-year-olds.
- UF6A- UF6H (TB)   Corresponding teacher guides.
- UF7A- UF7H (PB)   Eight text-books for 17-18-year-olds.
- UF7A- UF7H (TB)   Corresponding teacher guides.

Boyd, N. *The Challenge of God* (Dublin: Gill & Macmillan, 1994)
- CG

Brady, R. *The Christian Way* series (Dublin: Veritas, 1980-83)
- CW1PB   *The Christian Way 1* (Pupil-text)
- CW1TB   *The Christian Way 1* (Teacher-guide and resource material)
- CW2PB   *The Christian Way 2* (Pupil-text)
- CW2TB   *The Christian Way 2* (Teacher-guide and resource material)
- CW3PB   *The Christian Way 3* (Pupil-text)
- CW3TB   *The Christian Way 3* (Teacher-guide and resource material)

Chadwick, O., *A History of Christianity* (London: Weidenfeld & Nicolson, 1995)
- HC

Combat Poverty, *Fair Shares?* (Dublin: Combat Poverty, 1991)
- FS

Dardis et al., *In Words and Deeds* (Dublin: Irish Jesuit/NCPI/ CAI/Trócaire 1991)
- WD

Duffy, C. *Religion for Living* series (Tara: Hawthorn Publishing,1994)
- RFL 1   *Religion for Living, Workbook 1*
- RFL 2   *Religion for Living, Workbook 2*
- RFL 3   *Religion for Living, Workbook 3*

Fleming and O'Hara, *World Religions and Beliefs* (Dublin: Gill & Macmillan, 1995)
- WRB

Forristal, D. *The Christian Heritage* (Dublin: Veritas, 1976)
- CH

Greville, B. *You Gather A People: an approach to worship* (Dublin: Veritas, 1983) (*God and Man* series)
- YGP   Pupil-text
- YGPTB   Teacher's guide

Hyland, M., *The New Christian Way* series (Dublin: Veritas, 1991-93)
- LOAPB   *Love One Another*
- LOATB   *Love One Another* (Teacher's book)
- SUWPB   *Show Us the Way*

- SUWTB   *Show Us the Way* (Teacher's book)
- TLPB   *A Time to Live*
- TLTB   *A Time to Live* (Teacher's book)

Hyland, Browner, Looney, *WAZE* series (Dublin: Veritas/Kairos, 1994-95)
- WWTB   *Workways* (Teacher's book)
- PWTB   *Prayerways* (Teacher's book)
- LWTB   *Lifeways* (Teacher's book)
- JWTB   *Justways* (Teacher's book)

Kirwan, S. and Garland, L., *The Light of the World* series (Dublin: Gill & Macmillan, 1989)
- LW1PB   *A New Commandment*
- LW1TB   *A New Commandment* (Teacher's book)
- LW2PB   *Believe the Good News*
- LW2TB   *Believe the Good News* (Teacher's book)
- LW3PB   *Teach Me Your Ways*
- LW3TB   *Teach Me Your Ways* (Teacher's book)

Konstant, D., ed., *Religious Education for Secondary Schools* (London: Search Press, 1976)
- RESS

Larkin, T. and McAndrew, P., *The Gateway* series (Navan: Columban Fathers and Sisters, 1989)
- G1   *In God's Image*
- G2   *A New Earth*
- G3   *Cry of the Poor*
- G4   *Signs of the Times*
- G5   *A Spirit of Power*

McCarthy, Liam S., *Creating Space for RE: The Ballygall Project* (Dublin: Columba Press, 1986)
- CSRE

McKenna, J., *Moral Questions* (Dublin: School and College Publishing, 1992)
- MQ

McKenna, J., *The Living Faith* series (Dublin: Veritas, 1988-90)
- LF1, Module1   My Journey
- LF1, Module 2   My Choices
- LF1, Module 3   My Commitments
- LF1TB   Teacher's Handbook
- LF2, Module1   We Believe
- LF2, Module2   We Hope
- LF2, Module3   We Love
- LF2TB   Teacher's Handbook

Peelo, M., *Who Cares?* (Dublin: Crosscare, 1995)
- WC   Video; Teacher's notes; Students' texts and Handouts

Pennock, M., *Moral Problems: What Does a Christian Do?* (Notre Dame: Ave Maria Press, 1979)
- MPPB   Pupil-text
- MPTB   Teacher's manual

Pennock, M., *Your Church and You: History and Images of Catholicism* (Notre Dame: Ave Maria Press, 1984)
- YCAY

Ward, M., *Yes, you do count* (Dublin/Belfast: Churches' Peace Education Programme, 1995)
- YYDC   Teacher's book and Student's worksheets

Walsh, A., *Believing and Living* series (Dublin: Veritas, 1994-95)
- BL1   *Reason to Believe* (Pupil-text)
- BL1   *Reason to Believe* (Teacher's book)

NOTES

Introduction: Helping Faith to Mature
1. See D. Lane, *The Experience of God,* chapter 3, 'The Activity of Faith' (Dublin: Veritas, 1981).
2. See L.McKenzie, *Christian Education in the Seventies,* chapter 2, 'The Aims of Christian Education' (New York: Alba House, 1971).
3. Mt 7:21.
4. Jm 1:22. See the letter of the Archbishop of Dublin on the occasion of the Crosscare annual collection, 17 September 1995: 'The celebration of our Sunday Mass challenges us not just to listen to the Gospel of love and justice but to take it to heart and so be doers of the word as well as hearers'.
5. J. Ratzinger, *Introduction to Christianity,* talks about 'The Creed as Expression of the Structure of the Faith' (pp. 56-64) (London: Search Press, 1971).
6. J. Macquarrie, in *Thinking about God,* wisely remarks that 'we could not think of God apart from the possibility of prayer to him' (p.108)(London: SCM, 1975).
7. J. Mackey, in *The Problems of Religious Faith,* talks about faith, charity and hope as 'the three phases through which religious faith passes' (p.261) (Dublin: Helicon, 1972).
8. See K. Nichols, *Cornerstone,* chapter 8, 'The Way Ahead' (Slough: St Pauls, 1978).
9. For an analysis of the concept 'education of the faith', see R. Rummery, *Catechesis and Religious Education in a Pluralist Society,* pp. 108-118 (Sydney: EJ Dwyer, 1975).

Chapter 1: Praying to the Father with Thanks
1. CCC refers to *The Catechism of the Catholic Church.* TYMB refers to P. M. Devitt, *That You May Believe: A Brief History of Religious Education* (Dublin: Dominican Publications, 1992).

2. See D. Lane, *Foundations for a Social Theology* (Dublin: Gill & Macmillan, 1984). See also R. Avila, *Worship and Politics* (New York: Orbis, 1981).
3. T. Balasuriya, *The Eucharist and Human Liberation* (London: SCM, 1979), p. 45.
4. Ibid.
5. See The Irish Bishops, *The Work of Justice* (Dublin: Veritas, 1977).
6. See K. Zappone, *The Irish Catechist,* vol. 8, no. 2, 'Sacramental Catechesis and the Spirituality of Liberation Theology'. See also M. Fox, *On becoming a Musical, Mystical Bear (Spirituality American Style)* (New York: Paulist Press, 1976), which links mysticism and prophecy around the image of *'radix'* or root. Mysticism and prayer imply becoming rooted in and enjoying life to the full. Prophecy involves uprooting all that threatens life, so that life can be shared justly (p. 73). See also D. Hay, 'Suspicion of the Spiritual: Teaching Religion in a World of Secular Experience', *British Journal of Religious Education (BJRE)* 7(3), 1985, pp. 140-147.
7. *The Didache,* chapter 7, in *Ancient Christian Writers,* vol. 6 (Washington: Catholic University of America Press, 1948). See also W. Cosgrave, 'Christian Spirituality Today', *The Furrow* (September 1995), pp. 501-509, in which he talks about 'the proper balance in one's own spiritual life between moral living and prayer'.
8. See M. Fox, *The Living Light,* 1975, no. 2, 'The Prayer and Spirituality of Jesus'.
9. For a simple explanation, see R. Reichert, *Teaching Sacraments to Youth* (New York: Paulist Press, 1975).
10. See G. Moran's treatment of this theme in *God Still Speaks* (London: Search Press, 1967), chapter 8.
11. The title of an article by B. Cooke in *Emerging Issues in RE* (ed. Durka and Smith) (New York: Paulist Press, 1976).

12. See D. Power, *The Living Light,* 1979, no. 2, 'The Mystery which is Worship'.
13. See *Constitution on the Liturgy,* par.10.
14. J. A. T. Robinson, *Honest to God* (London: SCM[15] 1971), p. 90, maintains that 'the test of worship is how far it makes us more sensitive to the "beyond in our midst", to the Christ in the hungry, the naked, the homeless and the prisoner'.
15. The developmental nature of faith and its sacraments is well explored in C. O'Donnell, *The Irish Catechist,* Vol. 6, no. 2, 'Ongoing Initiation'. See also Somerville, *The Sower,* October 1973, 'Sacraments: Celebration of Life'.
16. For a list of prayers in the *Children of God* series, see Sean Melody, *Leading our Children to God,* pp. 62-63; also M. Hyland, *The Children of God,* pp. 9-14.
17. *Catechesi tradendae* 67.
18. In *The Irish Catechist* vol. 7, no. 2 (1983), p. 61, Ray Brady claims that 'certain components of catechesis are at best marginalised in the school situation…. Prayer, liturgy, personal encounter don't easily find a place in our classrooms.' One might suggest here that it is precisely the *study of religion* which ought to occupy this place in class. In fact, with such study in mind, Kirwan and Garland, in their *Light of the World* series, offer material on the 'Liturgical Year' (unit 7) and 'Worship and Prayer' (unit 8) in *LW1PB* (for an explanation of this and other shorthand references, see the list of *textbooks consulted*) pp. 88 ff. In the *New Christian Way* series, by M. Hyland, Book One (*Love One Another*) offers 'A Time to Pray' in the pupils' book (*LOAPB,* p. 12); 'Stations of the Cross' in the teacher's book (*LOATB,* p. 80); and 'Appendix 2: Songs and Hymns in *LOATB,* p.111. See also the liturgical resource material in *LOATB,* 43; *LOAPB,* 45; and *LOAPB,* 170. At senior level there is a textbook called *You Gather a People* (subtitled *An Approach to Worship*). The author, Sister Brid Greville, states that 'the purpose of the book is to evoke in young people today

a deeper *understanding* of worship and a desire to communicate with God – both alone and with others' (p. 1). An attempt is made to outline a systematic sacramental catechesis for young adolescents which recognises 'the role of the sacraments in the formation of faith' (this is the title of an article by W. Bausch in *The Living Light*, 1977, no. 2). The importance of making a serious study of the worship dimension of faith is highlighted dramatically in *Understanding Faith: Religious Education in the Catholic Secondary School (UF)*. This 1991 Aotearoa/New Zealand syllabus has a 'scope and sequence chart' for each year, which shows how each of the eight topics studied in each year relates to a range of concerns (human experience, doctrine, Scripture, Church, **Worship/Sacraments,** Christian existence, universal religious dimension). John McKenna's *Living Faith (LF)* series has regular sections called 'Prayer response', 'Pause for prayer', and 'Time for reflection' (see his *LF1PB*). *LF2TB*, p. 19, states that 'most units contain material for prayer/reflection'. Another very helpful resource is Hyland, Browner and Looney, *Prayerways (PW)*, which attempts 'to explore the place of prayer in the lives of the students, to examine our rich heritage of prayer, the context and content of Christian prayer' (p. 5). Of particular interest in this teacher's book are the many quotations concerning prayer that are taken from the Catechism of the Catholic Church; also the section 'What's in a Building?' (pp. 61-74) and the range of prayer services in pp. 88-107. Note how worship (prayer, liturgy) is *studied* and not just exercised (said, celebrated).

Chapter 2: Knowing God More Clearly

1. See S. M. de Benedittis, *Teaching Faith and Morals* (Minneapolis: Winston Press, 1981), chapter 2, 'Catechesis for Understanding the Message.' See also J. Astley, 'The Place of Understanding in Christian Education and Education about Christianity', *BJRE* 16(2), 1994, pp. 90-101.

2. G. Baum, *Faith and Doctrine* (New York: Paulist Press, 1969), p. 14, refers to 'faith as new consciousness'.
3. D. Murray, *Jesus is Lord* (Dublin: Veritas, 1973), p. 10.
4. See G.K.Chesterton, *Orthodoxy* (London: Fontana², 1963), p.46: 'tradition is only democracy extended through time'.
5. See J. Wilcken, *The Gospel and the Church's Teaching Role* (Melborne: Polding Press, 1977), p. 67, where he suggests that 'when we are too eager to attribute absoluteness to our statements we are in danger of divinising them'.
6. K. Nichols, *Truth and Consequences* (Essex: Kevin Mayhew, 1977), makes the point (p.7) that 'education in doctrine is to help people get inside their tradition'.
7. See G. Vermes, *Jesus the Jew* (London: Fontana²,1977); and J. Meyer, *A Marginal Jew* (New York: Doubleday, 1991).
8. C. Dickens, *Hard Times,* chapter 1.
9. General Catechetical Directory, 21. An analysis of R. Brady's *The Christian Way (CW1)* will indicate how religious knowledge (in the first two senses) is of major concern. Chapter 6 aims at understanding the essential link between Jesus and the Eucharist. Chapter 8 gives information about Martin Luther's protest. Chapter 10 gives information about the beginnings of Jesus' ministry. Chapter 11 cultivates an awareness of the opposition to Jesus. Chapter 12 wants pupils to understand Jesus as servant of God and Chapter 14 offers knowledge of the Church's proclamation of the good news. In terms of the Irish language, these items are 'fios' and 'eolas' items, and are clearly the items that are given a special focus in second-level religion teaching. Connie Duffy's *Religion for Living* series explains the underlying process on the back page. Item 4 is called Check your Knowledge; Item 5 is called Check your Understanding; and Item 7 is called Religion Diary (this provides an opportunity for a personal response to the lesson). This series tries to assess both the factual and the systematic knowledge gained in class; while it also opens up

the possibility of personal knowledge being deepened. D. Forristal's *The Christian Heritage* (for suggestions as to its use, see the article by G. Rice in *The Irish Catechist,* vol.6, no.1, 1982) is a senior-cycle textbook which attempts to banish many kinds of religious ignorance. It can help the religion teacher lead pupils out of the darkness of ignorance into the light of truth. Of course this requires that the good teacher constantly makes this journey afresh. Another similar textbook is M. Pennock, *Your Church and You,* subtitled 'History and Images of Catholicism'. See also Crawford and Rossiter's idea of the 'historical core curriculum' as outlined in *Missionaries to a Teenage Culture* (Sydney: Christian Brothers, 1988), chapters 17, 18. See also the Aotearoa/New Zealand syllabus, *Understanding Faith,* pp. 47-48 (*UF6C,* 'The Church's Story: The Modern Age'; and *UF6G,* 'Christian Art, Architecture, Music'). For an example of suitable material at senior level, see A. Walsh, *Believing and Living series, BL1, Reason to Believe,* Chapters 6-10, especially chapter 10 entitled 'Christianity'; and also *BL1, Reason to Believe,* 'Evil and Suffering and the Challenge to Christian Faith' (chapter 13); and the New Zealand *Understanding Faith* (*UF7G* 'Jesus the Christ – A critical historical study'; and *UF7H,* 'Mary, the First Disciple'). An excellent resource for teachers of religion at any level is the classic study by Owen Chadwick, *A History of Christianity* (London: Weidenfeld & Nicolson, 1995). This explains how Christianity interacted with and had a great influence on all aspects of human culture with which it came into contact.

10. Andrew McGrady has a different way of analysing 'religious knowing'. It comprises what he calls 'religious behaviour' (acting); 'religious feeling' (sentiment); and 'religious understanding' (thinking). In my analysis, 'personal knowledge' comprises both acting and sentiment; while 'factual' and 'systematic knowledge' together are what

McGrady calls thinking or 'religious understanding'. Michael Paul Gallagher's analysis of faith as 'hand', 'heart', and 'head' relates as follows to Mc Grady's analysis: acting = hand; sentiment = heart; thinking = head.

11. See J. Macquarrie, *Thinking about God* (London: SCM, 1975), chapter 11, 'The Nearer Side of God', which explores some biblical images of the Spirit.
12. See J. McKenna, *The Living Faith 2* (Teacher's Book, pp. 80-81): 'In the Name of the Bee'. See also B.Watson, *Education and Belief* (Oxford: Blackwell, 1987), pp. 166-169, in a chapter on conceptual development and RE, 'The Present, the Ball and the Import'; and H. Reich, 'Can one Rationally Understand Christian Doctrines? An Empirical Study', *BJRE* 16 (2), 1994, pp. 114-126.
13. See E.A. Robinson, 'RE: A Shocking Business', in *New Directions in RE* (Sussex: Falmer Press, 1982), ed. J.Hull.
14. This word is a personal creation. It echoes other words such as 'literate' or 'numerate.'
15. Augustine of Hippo, *De Catechizandis Rudibus,* chapter 6. See *Ancient Christian Writers*, vol. 2, ed. Quasten/Plumpe (London: Longman Green^2, 1952)

Chapter 3: Looking at Life through the Eyes of Christ

1. See A. Exeler, 'Catechesis as the Proclamation of a Message and the Interpretation of Experiences', *Lumen vitae*, 1970, no. 4.
2. K. Nichols, *Cornerstone* (Slough: St Pauls, 1978), talks about 'the educated Christian' as a person of 'discernment: the ability to see and understand secular life in the light of the Gospel' (p. 35).
3. For an outline of the critical, prophetic perspectives of feminist consciousness, see A. L. Gilligan, 'Feminist Theology: The Interweaving of Method and Content', *The Irish Catechist,* vol. 8, no. 3. For a critical view of the whole

Catholic Church world-wide, see the works of J. Dunn, *No Lions in the Hierarchy* (Dublin: Columba Press, 1994) and *No Vipers in the Vatican* (Dublin: Columba Press, 1996).
4. M. Harris, 'Word, Sacrament, Prophecy', in *Tradition and Transformation in RE,* ed. P. O'Hare (Birmingham, Alabama: RE Press, 1979), p. 48.
5. K. Rahner, *The Shape of the Church to Come* (London: SPCK[2], 1975), pp. 123-132. See also P.McVerry, 'The Church must take sides', *The Furrow* (February 1993), pp. 78-83; and J.O'Brien, *Seeds of a New Church* (Dublin: Columba Press, 1994).
6. See the (as yet unpublished) *Progress Report on Adult Religious Education Project,* submitted by M. Kennedy to the Irish Bishops' Catechetics Commission, 1997.
7. For an examination of the relation of leisure to schooling see G. Moran, 'Leisure: A New Problem', in *Sign 58,* no.10 (1979), pp. 10-14; see also P. M. Devitt, *How Adult is Adult Religious Education?* (Dublin: Veritas, 1991), pp. 240-247.
8. See R. Reichert, *A Learning Process for Religious Education* (Dayton: Pflaum Publishing, 1975), and also P. M. Devitt, *That you may Believe* (Dublin: Dominican Publications, 1992), pp. 93-113.
9. See T. Groome, *Christian Religious Education* (San Francisco: Harper & Row, 1980). See also G. Durka, 'Christian Nurture and Critical Openness', *Lumen vitae* (1981), no.3.
10. See R. Brady, *The Christian Way* series (*CW3, chapter 5*). All the best religion texts now in use have taken to heart the prophetic dimension of faith. See M. Hyland, the *revised CW3, (A Time to Live),* pp. 175-178 'Prophets who seek Justice'; and pp. 215-217 'Responding to Poverty'. See also Kirwan& Garland's *LW 3 (Teach me your Ways),* chapter 19, 'Prophets', and see also *Understanding Faith* 7C (Biblical Studies 2, 'Amos and Jonah'). Larkin & McAndrew *GATEWAY 4 (Signs of the Times)* is a manual for religious

education on the theme of culture. It encourages photocopying (is teacher friendly), uses a version of Groome's shared praxis approach, offers lists of resources (books, videos, addresses of agencies), and provides good material for a critical analysis of the mass media (pp. 46-60) and ecology (p. 45).
11. See Molière's play, *Tartuffe*, or the film *Jesus of Montreal*, where these themes are beautifully explored on stage and screen.
12. T. Fleming, 'Education for Dissent', *The Irish Catechist*, vol. 8, no. 1.
13. See J. Chittister, *The Fire in these Ashes* (Leominster: Gracewing, 1996).

Chapter 4: Building the future in Hope
1. A. Toffler, *Future Shock* (London: Pan Books, 1972), p. 11.
2. For example, J. Moltmann, *Theology of Hope* (London, SCM[3], 1970). See also J. Macquarrie, *Thinking about God* (London: SCM, 1975), chapter 20, 'Theologies of Hope: a critical examination'; D. Lane, 'In Search of Hope', *Doctrine and Life* (December 1993), pp. 598-610, and *Keeping Hope Alive* (Dublin: Gill & Macmillan, 1996); and W. Riley, *The Spiritual Adventure of the Apocalypse: What is the Spirit saying to the Churches?* (Dublin: Dominican Publications, 1997).
3. H. Küng, *Eternal Life?* (London: Collins, 1984), p. 120.
4. T. Groome, *Christian Religious Education*, pp. 15, 21.
5. A. Greeley, *The Great Mysteries* (Dublin: Gill & Macmillan, 1977), p. 12.
6. H. Küng, op. cit., p. 149.
7. M. Hellwig, *Tradition: The Catholic Story Today* (Dayton: Pflaum Publishing, 1974), p. 87.
8. See E. McDonagh, 'Hope: Going Forward to Christ', in *Truth and Life* (Dublin: Gill & Macmillan, 1969).
9. See D. Lane, 'Jesus and the Kingdom of God', *The Living*

Light, 1982, no. 2, for the notion of 'the creative power of the future' (p. 111).
10. See D.Lane, *Keeping Hope Alive*, p. 183, where he talks about the humanity of Jesus as 'a humanity deeply immersed in the history of the cosmos and its galaxies...a history rooted in the history of humans and their radical relationality'.
11. G. Moran, *Vision and Tactics* (London: Burns & Oates, 1968), p. 110.
12. K. Rahner clarifies the nature of Christian hope in *Theological Investigations* vol. 6 (London: DLT, 1974): 'Marxist Utopia and the Christian future of Man'.
13. G. Moran, op.cit., chapter 7.
14. A. Greeley, *The Great Mysteries*, op. cit. p.21.
15. H. Küng, op. cit., p. 287.
16. J. Mackey, *Problems of Religious Faith* (Dublin: Helicon, 1972), pp. 303-314.
17. I am indebted for this analysis to a masterly talk given by Richard Hayes in the Mater Dei Institute in February 1997.
18. For an alternative reading of 'inner' Church history, through recounting the stories of outstanding saints, see T. Tilley, *Story Theology*, chapter 8, 'The Body of Christ', pp. 147-181.
19. See D. Konstant (ed.), *Religious Education for Secondary Schools* (London: Search Press, 1976) *(RESS)*.
20. See R. Brady, *The Christian Way, Book 1 (CW1TB)*, p.108. See also the following reflection: 'What the Christian enjoys now as God's grace he has as pledge and promise of eternal glory. So, in spite of sin and its several manifestations, the Christian dares to hope' (ibid., p. 134).
21. See M. Hyland, *New Christian Way 3*, Lesson 22, 'Looking to the Future' (Heaven and Hell); also Kirwan, Garland, *Light of the World 3*, chapter 24 'Jesus' Resurrection', chapter 25 'The Last Things'; J. McKenna, *Living Faith 2:* 'WE HOPE' (*passim*); A. Walsh, *Reason to Believe* (Book 1 of the *Believing and Living* series): chapter 11, The Foundations of Christian

Faith, chapter 12, The Challenge of Christian Faith, chapter 13, Evil and Suffering and the Challenge to Christian Faith, chapter 14, 'If Christ has not been raised from the dead your faith is in vain'; the New Zealand series *Understanding Faith 7B: Sects, Cults, and New Religious Movements*; Larkin, Mc Andrew *Gateway 5, A Spirit of Power,* Part 7, 'Shaping the Future Now', p.34; and N. Boyd, *The Challenge of God,* Part 4, Human Destiny (ageing, the reality of death, coping with grief, dying with dignity, life after death?, near death experiences, the life beyond the grave).

Chapter 5: Changing Radically under the Spirit's Inspiration

1. E. McDonagh, article in *Truth and Life,* pp. 24-38. For a penetrating analysis of this and other possible approaches to moral thinking, see D. Harrington, *What is Morality?* (Dublin: Columba Press, 1996)
2. See D. Murray, *Jesus is Lord,* chapter 4, 'Return to Me'.
3. See Lamarche, 'The Call to Conversion and Faith', *Lumen vitae,* 1970, no. 2.
4. See J. Mackey, *The Problems of Religious Faith,* pp. 250-266.
5. See M. Maher, 'Abraham our Father in Faith', in *When God Made a Promise* (Manchester: KOINONIA, 1976).
6. K. Rahner reminds us, in *Do You Believe in God?* (New York: Paulist Press, 1969), p. 107, that faith 'remains God's grace'.
7. See H. Lombaerts, 'Aims of a Catechesis on the Eucharist', *Lumen vitae,* 1969, no. 3.
8. Many catechetical journals have explored this theme. See especially *The New Sower,* winter 1975-76; *Lumen vitae,* 1982, no. 2; *The Irish Catechist,* 1982, no. 4; *The Living Light,* March 1984.
9. M. Harris (ed.), *Parish Religious Education* (New York: Paulist Press, 1978), p. 13.
10. *Evangelii nuntiandi,* 41.

11. See B.Watson, *Education and Belief* (Oxford: Blackwell, 1987), pp. 13, 105.
12. See J. Joyce, *A Portrait of the Artist as a Young Man* (Middlesex: Penguin, 1973), p. 119.
13. See R. Brady, *The Christian Way* series, Book 3 *(CW3)*. All the religion textbooks now in use also have a major moral component. See M. Hyland's *TLTB*, Unit 6: Living for the Kingdom; Unit 8: Called to live and love. See also Kirwan and Garland, *LW1*, Unit 2: Love/Refusing to love (includes making choices); also chapter 17, A New Commandment; *LW2*, Unit 1: Stewards of God's Creation (Freedom, making decisions); also chapter 14, Call and Response; *LW3*, Unit 1: Beliefs and Values, Unit 2: Christian Beliefs and Values, Ch 23: Beatitudes. See J. McKenna, *LF1*(2) 'My choices', *LF2*(3) 'We Love', and *Moral Questions* (new edition). See N. Boyle, *The Challenge of God*, Part 3 (Morality). See C. Duffy, *Religion for Living 2*, Unit 11 (Making the right decisions); *Religion for Living 3*, Unit 11 (Respect for Life). See *UF5B*, 'Conscience, Morality and Values'; and *UF6F*, 'Christian Morality and Moral Development'. See Hyland, Browner, Looney, *Lifeways*, which deals with issues of sexuality and relationships for senior pupils. It draws upon the pastoral letter, *Love is for Life*. The material is graded as follows: very easy, easy and more advanced.
14. See M. Pennock, *Moral Problems* (Notre Dame: Ave Maria Press, 1979).
15. See *The Religious Dimension of Education in a Catholic School* (Dublin: Veritas, 1988), 51-65.
16. An example of what I mean is the collection of *Irish Times* articles in N. O'Faoláin, *Are you Somebody?* (Dublin: New Island Books, 1996), part 2, 'Selected Journalism' (people, the times, issues and belief), pp. 205-351.
17. ibid. p.340.

Chapter 6: Building Community
1. See K. Rahner, 'Theological Justification of the Church's Developmental Work', *Theological Investigations* Vol. 20, which speaks about 'man's socio-political and socio-critical task' (p. 69).
2. See J. Arias, *Give Christ Back to Us* (Dublin: Mercier Press, 1974), p. 95.
3. G. Guttierez, *A Theology of Liberation* (London: SCM, 1974), p. 194, claims that 'to know God is to do justice'.
4. Jn 17:21.
5. H. Küng, *On Being Christian* (London: Collins, 1976), p. 251.
6. D. Lane, 'Jesus and the Kingdom of God', *The Living Light*, 1982, no. 2, p. 111.
7. R. Kearney, 'God', *The Furrow*, December 1984, asserts that 'God's creation cannot be completed without man's creative intervention' (p. 750).
8. See S. McDonagh, 'Eucharist and Creation', *Doctrine and Life* (July/August 1995), pp. 420-427.
9. Title of chapter 7 of D. Murray, *Jesus is Lord*. For an excellent summary of recent Church teaching on social issues, in a form accessible to school work, see *Understanding Faith* 6 B, pp. 21-27. See also J. Kavanagh, 'Rerum Novarum', *The Furrow* (April, 1992), pp. 215-221; and K. O'Rourke, 'An Economist looks at Catholic Social Teaching', *Doctrine and Life* (July/August 1995), pp. 405-413.
10. See also *The Religious Dimension of Education in a Catholic School*, pars.88-90; *Understanding Faith* 6B, pp. 7-12; and C. Mangan, 'Creation Texts of the Bible', *Doctrine and Life* (March 1995), pp. 216-224.
11. P. Kirby, *Lessons in Liberation* (Dublin: Dominican Publications, 1981), chapter 3, is called 'Conscientisation: Insisting on Truth'.
12. *Gaudium et spes,* 34.

13. Ibid., 33.
14. R. Kearney, op.cit., p. 744, talks about the power of God as *dunamis* or potency or possibility.
15. *Gaudium et spes*, 34.
16. Ibid., 21.
17. Ibid., 43.
18. M.Hellwig, *What are the Theologians Saying?* (Dayton: Pflaum/Standard, 1970), p. 87.
19. H. Küng, *Eternal Life?* (London: Collins, 1984), p. 247.
20. The Irish Bishops, *The Work of Justice*, p.5. See also Sean Brady, 'Working for Justice', *The Furrow* (June, 1995), pp. 339-348.
21. *Gaudium et spes*, 43.
22. See also P. Babin, *Options* (London: Burns & Oates[2], 1969), chapter 5 of which is entitled 'Commitment to the World' (pp. 118-129).
23. *Gaudium et spes*, 57.
24. S. Healy and B. Reynolds, *Social Analysis in the Light of the Gospel* (Maynooth: Kairos, 1983), p. 82, makes the point that 'our ultimate aim is to develop effective, relevant Gospel-based action'.
25. J. Holland and P. Henriot, *Social Analysis* (Maryknoll, NY: Orbis/Center of Concern, 1983), is subtitled 'Linking Faith and Justice'.
26. K. Rahner, *Theological Investigations,* Vol. 10, 'The Peace of God and the Peace of the World'.
27. H. Küng, op. cit., p. 40.
28. *1000 Quotable Poems,* Vol. 1, p. 120, compiled by R. C. Clark (New York: Bonanza Books, 1985).
29. See R. Brady, *The Christian Way,* Book 3. See also *Workways* (Hyland, Browner, Looney), a pack for senior-cycle pupils which invites them 'to explore the reality of unemployment in the world today, to examine some of the issues raised in the pastoral *Work is the Key…*'. For a good treatment of the

themes of human dignity and freedom, see *Understanding Faith* 6B, pp. 37-44. For a good, simple treatment of human rights and justice, suitable for Junior Certificate pupils, see Duffy, *RFL3* Units 7 and 9. See also McCarthy's *Creating Space for RE,* p.56: 'Christians and the Third World'; and Kirwan and Garland's *LW3,* chapters 5 (human rights); 6 (travellers); and 7 (developing world).
30. See M. Sawicki, *The Gospel in History* (New York: Paulist Press, 1988).
31. See *CSRE,* p. 31 (Contact Session).
32. See M.Pennock, *Moral Problems,* p. 154. See also C. Duffy's *RFL2* Lessons 11-13 (Care for the Earth, St Francis, Tree of Life). See also *Gateway 3 (Cry of the Poor),* p. 5; *Gateway 5 (A Spirit of Power)* p. 5; *LF1*,2 pp. 120, 127; Crosscare video and pack, a programme for Transition Year and Senior Cycle, entitled *Who Cares?; Understanding Faith* 6B, pp. 34-36 (A Method for Action).
33. See the Combat Poverty resource material called *Fair Shares?* and also Dardis et al., *In Words and Deeds;* and see also M. Ward, *Yes, you do Count; A Teaching Programme on Human Rights.* See T. Duffy, 'Teaching Peace in Northern Ireland', *The Furrow* (March 1994), pp. 163-169; and also the eleven chapters of *Understanding Faith* 6B (justice and peace); also LF2, 2, 'We Hope'; and G2, 'A New Earth'.
34. Nerissa, *The Merchant of Venice,* Act 1, Scene 2.

Chapter 7: Working for Christian Unity
1. See W. Murphy, 'The Ecumenical Dimension of Catechesis', *The Irish Catechist,* Vol.1, no. 2.
2. *Catechesi tradendae,* 32.
3. Two new encyclical letters *Orientale lumen* and *Ut Unum Sint,* address the challenges facing ecumenism today. Commenting on them in the *Tablet* (21 October 1995), Cardinal König says that they 'show how greatly ecumenical concern is emphasised

and promoted by the head of the Catholic Church. The commitment at base remains feeble, however'.
4. E. McDonagh, 'Theology and Irish Divisions', *The Furrow*, January 1979, pp. 24, 25. It is encouraging to realise that some learning along these lines has been taking place since McDonagh's words were written. Recently the Dublin Archdiocese celebrated ten years of the process called Parish Development and Renewal (PDR). In this process the emphasis is on collaborative ministry by all the believers in a parish. For a theological analysis of this process, see D. Harrington, *Parish Renewal* (1997) (Dublin: Columba Press, 1997).
5. It is worth noting here that *Catechesi tradendae* is even stronger on this point: 'it is extremely important to give a correct and fair presentation of the other Churches and ecclesial communities that the Spirit of Christ does not refrain from using as means of salvation' (32).
6. D. Lane in *The Future of Religion in Irish Education*, (Dublin: Veritas, 1997).
7. The new Catechism has a clearly Trinitarian tone. For an explanation of some of the implications of a Trinitarian faith, see articles by E. Cassidy, 'I Believe – We Believe' (pp. 27-38), and by B. Leahy, 'The Profession of the Christian Faith' (pp. 39-47) in P. M. Devitt (Ed.), *A Companion to the Catechism* (Dublin: Veritas, 1995).
8. Cyril of Jerusalem, *Catechesis*, no. 10, par. 5, in *Fathers of the Church,* vols 61, 64 (Washington: Catholic University of America Press, 1970).
9. A. Greeley, *The Great Mysteries* (Dublin: Gill & Macmillan, 1977), p.xvii.
10. See E. McDonagh, op.cit., p. 26. It is this spirit of openness towards other Christian traditions which inspires the ecumenical content of most modern second-level Catholic Religion text-books. Examples would be the following – M. Hyland, *SUW* Lesson 15: We are all different; *TL* Lesson 12:

The Orthodox Church; C. Duffy, *RFL2* Lesson 21: A Protestant Church, Lesson 22: Christians Together, *RFL3* Unit 6: The Orthodox Church; Kirwan and Garland: *LW1* chapter 33: Ecumenism, *LW2* chapter 33: Some Christian Denominations (C. of I.; Methodists; Presbyterians), chapter 34: Orthodox Church, chapter 35: Christian Unity, *LW3* chapter 33: Ecumenism (Taize). See also *Understanding Faith 5E*: 'Ecumenism and Catholic Identity'. All of this material has a simple objective, well expressed by R. Brady, as follows: 'The important thing is to aim at some development of understanding. Understanding the original impetus, the present impasse; understanding how much Christians have in common; understanding the non-religious forces of division' (CW1TB, p. 8).

11. See R.E. Brown, K.P. Donfield and J. Reumann (eds.), *Peter in the New Testament* (London: Geoffrey Chapman, 1974), for an exploration of the common ground between Catholics and Lutherans regarding the Petrine ministry. See also Yarnold and Chadwick, *An ARCIC Catechism* (London: Incorporated Catholic Truth Society, 1983), for a brief summary of the situation between Anglicans and Roman Catholics. A recent book which surprises many is J. Macquarrie, *Mary for All Christians* (London: Collins, 1991). Christians of all major traditions share together in the modern appreciation of Celtic Spirituality. The roots of this spirituality in Druidic religion and also in Eastern Orthodox monasticism are recognised by all as hope for future ecumenical unity.

12. A. Falconer, *The Furrow,* January 1983, pp. 35-42.

13. J. Ledwidge, 'Ecumenism: A Way Ahead?', *The Irish Catechist,* March 1982. Catechists need much resource material to build up their own store of ecumenical knowledge. For helpful background reading, see T. Ware, *The Orthodox Church* (Middlesex: Penguin, 1993); M. Hurley,

Theology of Ecumenism (Dublin: Mercier Press, 1969) and Vatican II's *Decree on Ecumenism;* A. Falconer, 'Towards Reconciling Reformed and Roman Catholic', *Doctrine and Life* (May/June 1993), pp. 274-286; P. Jacob, 'What Friends Believe', *The Furrow* (September 1993), pp. 490-492; J. Thompson, 'A Presbyterian Viewpoint', *The Furrow* (July/August 1993), pp. 399-402; J. Neill, 'The Church of Ireland Way', *The Furrow* (May 1993), pp. 283-287; and R. Dunlop, 'Baptists: People of the Third Way', *The Furrow* (April 1993), pp. 226-229, as well as *A Precarious Belonging* (Belfast: Blackstaff Press, 1995), which documents the many problems of identity confronted by Irish Protestants today.
14. P. Mc Carthy, 'Twenty Ecumenical Questions, *The Furrow* (January 1997), pp. 3-6.
15. See Cyril of Jerusalem, *Catechesis* 4, op. cit.

Chapter 8: Sharing with all People

1. See P. Babin, *Options*, chapter 7, entitled 'The World View'. See also F. Sheeran, 'A Different Church', *The Furrow* (September 1995), pp. 475-482.
2. *Ad gentes,* 13.
3. K. Rahner, 'The Abiding Significance of the Second Vatican Council', *Theological Investigations,* Vol.20, p. 99, speaks of the 'optimism of universal salvation'. For a stimulating account of new missionary theology, see D. Bosch, *Transforming Mission* (Maryknoll, NY: Orbis, 1994). See also B. Hearne, 'New Models of Mission', *The Furrow* (February 1993), pp. 91-98.
4. For a treatment of Judaism see Klein, 'Catechetics and the Jews', *The Clergy Review* (September 1979); 'Judaism', *British Journal of Religious Education* (summer 1981); Kelly, 'Judaism and Christianity', *The Irish Catechist* (October 1982); 'Jewish Perspective on RE', *Religious Education* (spring 1983). *BJRE* also has features on Islam (autumn 1982) and Hinduism

(summer 1984). See also W. Haussman, 'Walking in other people's Moccasins?', *BJRE* 15(2), 1993, pp. 12-22; and P. and L. Connolly, 'Buddhism and the Religious Studies Approach to RE in the Secondary School', *BJRE* 9(1), 1986, pp. 27-33; M. Grimmitt, 'Religious Education and the Ideology of Pluralism', *BJRE* 16(3), 1994, pp. 133-147; M. Moore, 'Teaching Christian Particularity in a Pluralistic World', *BJRE* 17(2), 1995, pp. 70-83; Short and Carrington, 'Learning about Judaism', *BJRE* 17 (3), 1995, pp. 157-167; R. Fitzmaurice, 'Christianity and Islam: Co-operation or Conflict?', *Doctrine and Life* (December 1994), pp. 596-605; and B. Watson, 'Beyond Facts: The Coming Together of Religions', in *The Effective Teaching of RE* (London: Longman, 1993), pp. 108-126.

5. A very enriching way of studying the great world religions is to visit their places of worship and reflect on the experience. See R. Homan, 'Visiting Religious Buildings', *BJRE* 16(1), pp. 7-13. See also Kirwan and Garland, *Light of the World 3*, Teach me your Ways: Interviews with Irish Muslims (chapter 34); with Jewish Rabbi (chapter 34); and with Irish Buddhists (chapter 34). See also Maura Hyland, *A Time to Live,* Lesson 13 on Islam; and Connie Duffy, *Religion for Living* 1, Unit 3, The Old Testament (Abraham, Sarah, Ruth and David); *RFL2,* Unit 8, The Old Testament (Moses, The Passover, The Commandments); *RFL 3* Unit 3, 'The Old Testament' (Amos, Jeremiah) and Unit 8, Islam. See also B. O'Hara and E. Fleming, *World Religions;* and A. Walsh, *Reason to Believe (Believing and Living* series, Bk. 1), chapter 8 'World Religions Today' (Hinduism, Buddhism, Islam) and chapter 9 (Judaism). See also *Understanding Faith* 6A (Religions of the World).

6. See M. Ryan, *Another Ireland: An Introduction to Ireland's Ethnic-Religious Minority Communities* (Belfast: Stranmillis College Learning Resources Unit, 1997).